D1357516

THE LICENTIOUS SOLDIERY

The Licentious Soldiery

RUPERT CROFT-COOKE

BERKSHIRE COUNTY LIBRARY

LONDON   W. H. ALLEN   1971

© RUPERT CROFT-COOKE, 1971

PRINTED IN GREAT BRITAIN BY

ALDEN AND MOWBRAY LTD OXFORD

FOR THE PUBLISHERS

W. H. ALLEN & CO LTD

ESSEX STREET LONDON WC2r 3JG

BOUND BY

WM. BRENDON & SON LTD

TIPTREE

ISBN 0 491 00487 7

Oxfordshire WITHDRAWN FOR SALE 1 7 FEB 1986 N 50p Co. Libraries

Contents

Preliminary Note

In a book called *The Moon in My Pocket*, written and published ahead of its place in this sequence, but intended as part of it, I told how I purchased a horse-drawn living-waggon and spent the first months of the Second World War travelling across southern England with a young gypsy as my sole companion. This happy adventure ended in Worcestershire where I spent the early summer months of 1940 with another clan of gypsies who came there every year for the pea-picking. It ended abruptly when the fall of France and the actuality of Dunkirk made it clear to me that this was no time for collecting material for a book on gypsies or indeed for anything but securing the protection of a uniform as quickly as possible.

What follows here is not a 'war' book—the only fighting I saw was in Madagascar, and the only serious service was in India, and these are described in two other books in this series already published, *The Blood-Red Island* and *The Gorgeous East*. But it seems to me worth while to recall the humours and ineptitudes of training in Field Security, the experiences of a man who had hitherto lived almost without discipline being suddenly subject to it, the companionship and rigours of an all-male society in unaccustomed circumstances, the day-to-day incidents, small tragedies and ridiculous triumphs of Army life away from any front, the joys of scrounging comforts and pleasures by using one's wits, the realities of Combined Operations, training on a number of ships and being at last transported to South and East Africa, the Army life, in fact, of a very lucky soldier who had been accustomed in peacetime as a writer to notice small things of interest about him and kept his unfailing gusto whatever the circumstances. Few books about war service have time for these matters, the writer hurrying on to the real incident, the fighting and tragedy of war, but true to my intention in all these books to pick up the details which others find too trivial for recall, I aim at a realism which does not depend on broad effects or earth-shaking events.

The period covered is first from May 1940 till May 1942. The narrative omits the Madagascar campaign and continues from October 1942 till February 1943 when I left South Africa for India.

I do not apologize for having enjoyed the war but I hope this admission will not make me seem insensitive to the suffering of others. I went where I was sent and it was not my fault that I had a good time.

CHAPTER ONE

Pershore

[1]

LYING beside a wood fire at night in the gypsy encampment which was at the time my only home, I could feel the thump of the bombs falling on Birmingham or Coventry thirty miles away. In the glorious summer weather of 1940 and in the placid countryside around the Worcestershire town of Pershore the sound was muted to a dull echo, but it was insistent and menacing. The gypsies, a family of good Romani breeding named Lock, thought of their son who had already been called up, and I realized that I should have to join the Army.

It was no time for the defence of an ivory tower which had been my first preoccupation in peacetime. Such a defence cost too much now in time and effort. The maintenance of one's private identity in the face of almost universal conformism is always a worthwhile struggle, but not I thought while a direct seaborne invasion, the first to threaten the country since Napoleon's time, might start at any moment. Talk of flat-bottomed boats collected across the Channel appealed to my rather literal imagination and I looked for some sort of service which would not be too monotonous and regimental, but would not carry the responsibility of commissioned rank.

An infantry captain in the local pub said, "If I were you I'd join a thing called the Field Security Service." He had just come through Dunkirk and had been given leave. "I saw something of them in France. They seemed to enjoy themselves."

I asked what they did.

"Rush about on motor bikes and catch spies," he said.

It was almost the only information I had when I wrote to

9

the advertised address of the organization which became the
Field Security Wing of the Intelligence Corps and was told to
report for an interview at an office in Whitehall.

I left the gypsy encampment at daybreak having dug out
from my one suitcase my only presentable suit and travelled up
to London for the first time since the outbreak of war. With a
group of civilians—rather an educated lot, I thought ap-
prehensively—I was lectured by an elderly major on the work
of FS, then in a private interview gave my qualifications for it,
that I spoke several languages, knew Germany and had
travelled a good deal in Europe.

"OTC?" asked the Major.

"Yes, but more than twenty years ago," I said. I was
thirty-seven years old.

"You won't have to go into a training unit first, then. You
can go straight to Winchester."

I did not quite understand this but it sounded like a privilege.

"What happens now?" I asked.

"You go back to your home and wait."

"I haven't got a home. I packed up my flat when war broke
out."

The Major was not interested.

"You must be living somewhere," he pointed out impatiently.

"With gypsies. In Worcestershire."

He stuck to his point.

"You must have a postal address there?"

"Yes. The Star Tavern," I said, naming the pub at which
most of the gypsies foregathered in the evenings.

"Right. You'll get instructions there to go to the nearest
recruiting office and be attested. You'll be given your fare to
Winchester where you'll report to the Field Security Training
Centre."

"How soon will that be?"

"Impossible to say. Might be in a matter of days. Or it may
be a month or two."

I returned to Pershore and to the tent in an orchard which I shared with George Lock. The gypsies would soon be leaving for Herefordshire and the hop-picking, for they had their fixed annual route from one centre of piece-work to another. When they did so, I thought, I would move into the Star Tavern, if my papers had not come through; meanwhile I would enjoy the last few weeks with my friends.

[2]

Almost immediately I became aware of a sinister attitude of suspicion and hostility among the people of Pershore, at first veiled and whispering but becoming overt and confident as the weeks passed. They thought I was a spy.

At first this seemed silly and rather amusing and for a long time I did not take it seriously, perhaps because I had not learned then, through experience both macabre and uncomfortable, what popular prejudice and stupidity can do to the individual who makes light of them. It is only now, thirty years later, that I see the events of summer 1940 in the backward community of an agricultural area, a community isolated and given to inter-marriage and inbreeding, as potentially near danger, even tragedy.

It must be remembered that this was immediately after the fall of France, a peak season for spy scares in Great Britain. There were radio warnings of the Fifth Column and some very effective propaganda against careless talk. Signposts on the roads and name-plates on the stations had been removed as a precaution against parachutists; the Home Guard manned roadblocks and there were endless reports from well-meaning people about lights seen to flash on lonely hillsides, many of which still persisted after I had joined Field Security and learned to investigate them. The spy fever of the 1914-18 war, in which innocent lives were lost, did not quite repeat itself in 1940, because the metropolitan was more intelligent and less hysterical, but in districts like this it came near to doing so.

How it started to centre round me I do not know, but it is not difficult to guess. The gypsies themselves were alien and mysterious in the rustic mind, and a man, presumably of some education, who lived with them, sleeping on the ground in a gypsy tent, was doubly so. I had come from heaven-knows-where—no one had seen me arrive. Questions had been asked for some time before I learned of them from a bright and friendly barmaid at the Angel who gave me the gist of them.

I had been seen taking photographs, and my camera, a Kodak Retina, was German. I spoke foreign languages for I had been heard conversing with the gypsies in their own tongue. (This was flattering for all that was left of Romanes among the gypsies travelling in England was an extensive vocabulary.) I went to the pubs at night and played darts in order to converse with soldiers. I had lived in foreign parts. I had admitted to the ownership of an Opel car—kept out of sight, of course. I had an unusual dog, for my yellow Alsatian Dingo had become a 'German Police dog' in local minds. Most damning of all, I 'made notes' and 'did a lot of writing'.

The barmaid, who came from Birmingham, told me all this with merry scorn for the credulity of the locals but soon I found it was no joke. Conversations would cease abruptly as I entered a bar. Most of the Pershore men had known each other from childhood and freely exchanged stories of what was happening in France. But when a 'mysterious stranger' who lived with gypsies came among them, they began pointedly to talk about their crops. If they spoke to me at all it was to ask elaborately casual questions. Did I know Germany well? What did I think of Hitler? Was my father an Englishman? Where did I get my camera?

The trouble was, of course, that I was as interested as anyone in events across the Channel, and wanted to hear all I could from returning soldiers. I remember the occasion when the infantry captain I have quoted came into the farmers' bar at the Angel, the principal pub in the town, having just arrived by train. No one had had time to warn him about me, and as he happened to have had some experience of Field Security I took the opportunity of finding out all I could about the branch I should later join. Our conversation produced the most extraordinary effect on our listeners. Signals were made from across the room, throats were cleared every few moments in an effort to catch the officer's eye, loud conversations about the weather were started in vain, till at last an ingenious friend hurried up with the information that the indiscreet new arrival was wanted on the telephone. Once safely out of my presence, he was warned and when he returned he looked at me rather as Caesar must have eyed Brutus.

A local tradesman's son went a stage farther. He was among the last to cross from Dunkirk. I asked him what the beaches had been like. "I'll tell you what," he said. "Some of our chaps were in a café in France a few weeks ago when a stranger came up and asked them a lot of questions. But they weren't fools, you know. They soon had him taped. He was reported to the police and arrested. Turned out to be a spy. *He*"—the young man eyed me fiercely—"*he* was *shot*. And a damn good thing too!"

He swallowed his drink and hurried out of the bar with an air of having shown himself to be too astute for me. So I never heard his first-hand account of Dunkirk.

Then I began to find myself watched, even followed. I used to take a path that led along the river bank during the afternoon, a path which had been almost unused when I found it. I would look over my shoulder to see a very casual pedestrian who would stop to light his pipe when I lit a cigarette, who would find that he needed a rest whenever I did, seating himself under a tree when I lay stretched on the turf. And if I went out at night I would see heads bob up over hedges and hear whispers not far behind.

One of those most convinced that I was a spy was the farmer on whose land the waggons of the Locks had stood for many pea-picking seasons in succession. His name was Meikle, a somewhat aggressive and hard-faced character, shrewd in his profession but otherwise uncultured and not over-intelligent. One morning as I lay asleep and out of sight in the tent he passed the encampment and found Eliza Lock, who had returned for a moment from the pea-fields, emerging from her waggon.

"You'll get into trouble," he shouted. "You know you're keeping a spy here."

Eliza, gypsy-like and evasive, said, "Don't know anything about that."

"Well, you are. You'll have the police round soon."

"They can come," said Eliza. "My oldest boy's in the Army and I don't know what more they want."

"You shouldn't do it, Mrs Lock. Not on my ground. You don't know anything about this fellow, do you?"

Eliza made her all-purpose reply.

"He's *some* mother's son!" she said defiantly, on hearing which undeniable truth Meikle departed.

But his threat that the police would investigate was made good next day, a Sunday.

I remember the scene very well. We were lying under the trees by the two living-waggons, and had finished eating our Sunday dinner, for which Eliza proudly provided plates and knives and forks. ("We're not savages, you see," her husband used to say.) It was a warm June day and in other encampments in the orchard the gypsies were no less replete and restful. Young George Lock had gone a few yards apart to scrape his fiddle but the sound was no more disturbing than the insect buzz. Suddenly Dolly Lock called "Here come the *mushgros!*" which on other occasions in gypsy life might have sounded an alarm or been a rallying cry but among the law-abiding Locks roused only curiosity and irritation.

A sergeant and two policemen on bicycles came down the track from the farm buildings, and resting their cycles against a tree came over to us and asked to see our identity cards. Mine was in my pocket and I produced it without rising and the sergeant examined it in silence. After looking at the Locks' cards they all cycled away.

This was the first time since they had been issued with identity cards that my gypsy friends had been asked to produce them and they knew perfectly well what had caused it. They knew that I had brought trouble to them, but they did not resent this as *gorgios* would have done. They had inherited from nomadic generations a sense of hospitality to refugees which had made a gypsy camp in other centuries a safe refuge from the law and it still persisted in less persecuted times. Or perhaps they felt that having adopted me they were not going to be told by any 'bleeding gavver' that I should be abandoned. Whatever I had done to bring the police to the camp they were on my side, and quiet, thoughtful little remarks came from the adults.

"Don't you take any notice of that lot," said downright Eliza. "They don't know their arse from their elbow."

"You stay along with us, my Rubert," said Fred Lock. "You'll be all right along with us."

That evening in the Star Inn where the gypsies chiefly gathered I found myself an object of hospitality to them all, Lees, Fletchers and Smiths from other groups in the orchard.

"Have a drop of levinor along wi' me, my Rubert!"

"Have a drink now. Don't say no to me otherwise I shall be 'fended." They did not know what a spy might be but since the police were against me I was under their protection, such as it was.

But the thing was going too far and I went next morning to Pershore police station and saw the senior official, who was, I seem to remember, a chief inspector.

I thought at the time he was a level-headed and intelligent man. I told him the facts about myself and that I was waiting to be called up, ironically enough for that particular branch of the Army concerned with Security. He was polite but non-committal. What could he do? There was talk in the district—he did not deny it, but there was nothing he could do about it. One had these things in wartime. The fact that I was living with gypsies did not help, of course. I suppose now that his attitude was that of the traditional bureaucratic policeman towards anyone who has somehow, through whatever circumstances, become categorized as a suspect.

I went on to Cheltenham to see my solicitor and friend, H. F. Midwinter, who had in the past shown himself a sagacious and dependable ally. He was not very encouraging. A client of his was already interned in the Isle of Man on suspicions which he considered no less groundless.

Back in Pershore the situation grew intolerable. The damnable thing was that one had no means of fighting it. No one ever came out into the open and made an accusation. There was no case to answer. I could not go up to a group of whispering fruit-growers and say that they were making fools of themselves, that they could check on my identity and past history as they liked. I could not protest that this campaign was slanderous and silly, for there was no one to protest to. The murmurs and accusations were in the air, in the manner of people I met, in their eyes and tones—nothing answerable was ever said.

In one pub I used to play darts with a crowd of Sappers every evening and this must have led to another report, for one evening a ginger-haired sergeant, unknown to them or me, was introduced to me by the landlord whom he had interviewed. With lumbering attempts at tact he asked me a number of questions the drift of which I did not fully gather until many months later when I had joined Field Security and met a man from the Worcester Section who remembered the incident and told me that the sergeant had been sent to investigate.

[3]

It came to a climax on another Sunday which may have been

in July. I went down to Pershore as usual on the bicycle I had hired, but because it was raining I decided that instead of going back to the orchard for lunch I would walk up to the Angel and have the *table d'hôte*, which was pretty good. I did so, leaving my bicycle in the yard of the Star.

That was enough. From the Star spread a rumour that I had been 'taken off by the police'—there was my bicycle left behind to prove it. This set fire to the whole explosive mass of suspicion and resentment. Someone must have suggested, perhaps not seriously, that I had been arrested. Someone must have added that he had *seen* me arrested. In less than twenty minutes the news was through the town—it was true, I *was* a spy, the police had 'taken' me, I was going to be shot.

Pershore people whom I have seen since still remember that hour or two on a showery Sunday, in the week of Churchill's greatest fighting speech. Each says now that, of course, *he* never suspected me, but each tells me that his neighbours were jubilant, for had not all their suspicions been justified? Within an hour the accounts had gained all the circumstantial etceteras that they needed—the police had found photographs and plans in my room, I had been identified as a member of the SS, I had been dropped by parachute only a few days before I arrived in the town. There was such an orgy of wishful thinking, such invention of convincing touches, that no doubt could be left in any citizen's mind.

Meanwhile, unconscious of this, I was finishing an excellent lunch at the Angel, a hospitable little hotel at which I used to breakfast and bath every day. As I walked back to the Star I fancied I was causing some surprise, but I was accustomed by now to being scrutinized, and took no notice. Not until I reached the Locks' encampment did I hear what had happened. They were in a state both of indignation and relief. A farm labourer's wife had rashly crossed the field to tell the family that their friend, "who she'd always known was a German," had been "took up by the police." This is a fate only too common in Little Egypt, and the Locks, perhaps, were not so convinced

B

as they afterwards claimed to be that the woman was lying. But whatever they may have believed privately, they took the announcement as a direct personal insult, and shouting the most violent abuse at her visitor Eliza had run to her waggon— as she did invariably in such a crisis—for her rings.

Now, Eliza's rings were four, and were worn on the right hand, and I personally should be sorry if they were ever slipped on during a disagreement between Eliza and myself. The *gorgio* woman seemed to have shared this feeling, for before Eliza had come down the steps of the waggon she had covered half the distance to her cottage.

I was surprised to find that this incident virtually closed the matter. Because the alarmists on that particular occasion had been proved wrong, the whole story of the spy in the gypsy camp was seen as a fallacy. The logic of this seems a little faulty, but it worked. I was at least tentatively accepted in the gathering of farmers and tradesmen in the bar of the Angel every morning. But not until I came back to the town, by a singular chance, in uniform with other soldiers to vouch for me, were they, I think, quite sure.

[4]

The gypsies moved on for the hop-picking in Herefordshire. I watched their waggons pull out of the orchard and go creaking down the road to Ross-on-Wye. The bar of the Star Tavern was half-empty at night and unnaturally quiet now that Eliza Lock no longer sang *Nellie Dean*, cheered on by cries of 'Give it them, my Liza!' or unnecessary calls for 'Order!'

The little town of Pershore, full of variegated life in the times of fruit and pea-picking and the annual horse-fair, took on an autumnal air. Not only the gypsies with their waggons had departed but also the mob of tramps, urban down-and-outs, travellers and ex-convicts which in those days collected wherever there was profitable piece-work. There were no longer fights in the streets at night or songs shouted by groups returning by starlight to their tents. I had counted myself one of this raggle-taggle company and now felt abandoned and very lonely.

The Star Tavern, scene of saturnalian gatherings, centre of horse-dealing and hard drinking by the nomads, had become again a respectable inn used by the *gorgio* house-dwellers and field labourers, and the good people who kept it returned to the normal life of inn-keepers. They were glad to have me occupying one of their comfortable bedrooms and eating their simple food in solitude in the saloon bar, paying at what was then the handsome rate of four pounds a week. I used to walk by the river in the afternoon, watching the swans, and at night play darts or listen to one of Churchill's history-making broadcasts.

I still had Dingo, the yellow Alsatian who had shared my life in a remote Gloucestershire village, in Kent, in London, with the circus and among the gypsies. He was now my only companion since for the first time, in any circumstances I could remember, in any country in which I had settled, I made no friends. Perhaps it was because I was daily expecting orders to enlist or perhaps the staid people of Worcestershire seemed dull after the lively gypsies, but certainly I remained alone.

I wrote an essay called *The Finest Hour* which was never published because it attacked Baldwin so virulently that my agents thought it libellous. I wrote to friends, but nearly all of those who had meant most to me in the past were already in the services and had no time for chatty correspondence with a civilian. I was not, I think, much preoccupied with the war. Having signed what I took to be an undertaking to join the Army as soon as I was called, I was relaxed and immune from worry. I think there must have been many others who had this sense of relief when they put themselves under discipline in some unambitious capacity. The anxieties of civilians, the horrors of the radio news bulletin and newspaper, the critical consideration of strategy, the attempt to assess our chances of victory, the fear of military reverses, all died out, for concern with them was useless. This soothing fatalism lasted me throughout my Army life, or at least until I was commissioned and began to feel responsibility.

[5]

It was not until September that I was ordered to report at the Recruiting Office in Worcester for attestation on September 10. This uncharacteristic accuracy about the date comes from the fact that I still have a certified copy of my attestation and see that I swore 'by Almighty God that I will be faithful and bear true allegiance to His Majesty King George the Sixth, His Heirs, and Successors, and that I will, as in duty bound, honestly and faithfully defend His Majesty, His Heirs, and Successors, in Person, Crown, and Dignity against all enemies, and will observe and obey all orders of His Majesty, His Heirs and Successors, and of the Generals and Officers set over me'. This sonorous oath must have survived from the nineteenth century or earlier.

My actions in Worcester that day seem to me anomalous. I had been so much alone during the last weeks that I had not discussed my enlistment with anyone and I must have felt that the occasion demanded some recognition of my own. I went to a jeweller's and bought for myself a watch and a ring. I had never possessed a watch, depending on that fifth sense which is developed by all who do not carry watches. One sees a clock and without specially noting the time one is able to give it accurately for the next two or three hours, never being more than five minutes out, while on waking one gauges it without difficulty. But I felt that the Army might upset this and I purchased a plain gold wrist watch which I kept for twenty years. Why I bought a ring I don't quite know, for I had always

disliked jewellery on men. This was inoffensively plain with a
garnet, a 'Siamese ruby' the jeweller called it, in a strong
Victorian setting. I think I had an idea that in uniform I should
want some personal touch, a link with less regimented times of
freedom in dress.

At the recruiting station there was fuss about the fact that
'volunteers' were attested in the morning while the afternoons
were reserved for those considered apparently less admirable,
who had been 'called up'.

"If you don't mind being done with them we can enlist you
this afternoon," an official told me. This seemed to me so
ridiculous a distinction that I shocked him by laughing and
stripped off with a number of men of the thirty-one age group
who were being called up just then.

The last time I had undergone a medical examination was at
the age of nineteen when about to leave for Argentina, and I
had some of the same sensation of excitement and anticipation,
for I regarded joining the Army, believe it or not, as a kind of
adventure, a conception I was slow to relinquish and have never
entirely lost. I was diffident about this, telling myself it was a
piece of absurd romanticism, and of course confided it to no
one. Even my mother took it for granted—she already had
three sons and a daughter in uniform, for I was the last in my
family to succumb to the temptation and remained throughout
the war the junior in rank. But that I did so regard it I am
certain and I remember walking out of the recruiting office
feeling a changed man. Well, there was no harm in that. I did
not expect anyone else to be impressed.

[6]

Before I left for Winchester I had to part with Dingo. That
brave and beautiful creature has figured in three of these books

for he scarcely left my side during the eight years of his life.

I had been told that Our Dumb Friends League undertook the care of dogs for owners who wished to join the services and could provide no other home for them and I wrote to this benevolent institution to receive a friendly letter agreeing to keep Dingo till I was in a position to have him back. I arranged to send him by rail to the ODFL kennels—in Berkshire, I seem to remember, and he was to leave on the day following my visit to Worcester.

That morning I was approached by a Canadian woman who with her ten-year-old son was staying in the town. She had heard I was sending my dog to a home and offered to look after him for me. I explained that I did not want to leave him in private care for he would inevitably gain the affection of his guardians who might not like to part with him when the war was over. She replied that her name was Mrs Pearkes; she was the wife of Major-General Pearkes who was over here in command of the First Canadian Division, and that after the war she would go back to Canada and return the dog to me.

Dingo had already made friends with her small son and it seemed to me that in leaving him to the care of these kindly people I would be doing the best possible service to my dog, and I agreed to their proposal.

I will tell the end of the story here, though it did not come for two years. When I was given my first leave a few months later I went straight to Pershore to see Dingo before visiting my mother or any human friend. I found him fit and well cared for, and although he came at once to my call and stayed beside me for the hours I was in the place, I could see that he was happy in his new home. I never saw him again but in 1942 a letter from Mrs Pearkes caught up with me while I was in hospital in Madagascar, as disturbing letters in the Army always seemed to find one at the worst possible time and in the most unpleasant places. Mrs Pearkes informed me that she had left the house in Pershore and moved into a private hotel where dogs were not allowed, so rather than send Dingo to a home

she had had him 'painlessly destroyed'. I particularly noted that
'painlessly', but otherwise will make no comment, leaving it to
other dog-owners to imagine how I felt and still feel after
nearly three decades.

CHAPTER TWO

Winchester

[1]

I HAD never been in the city of Winchester but I imagined it to be a nice, scholarly, ecclesiastical sort of place among whose ancient buildings the training centre for counterspies would be discreetly set. I knew that my great-uncle George Crafter Croft had been senior science master at the college for many years and had been known as 'The Crafter' to generations of Wykehamists. He had occupied that post in the 1880s, Bosie Douglas's time, and died well within my own memory, and it gave me some link with the town. My instructions were to report at King Alfred's College—some mediæval foundation, I supposed, as I walked from the station to the Southgate Hotel for a last civilian drink before passing through its portals, which had to be fateful in my mind.

The proprietor of the Southgate, whom I came to know better in the months that followed, gave me little information that day.

"We get your fellows in here quite a lot," he said. "They seem a very nice crowd."

'Nice' was not quite the term I hoped to hear applied to my fellow trainees in defensive intelligence, but it was only too apt, as I was soon to discover.

King Alfred's College turned out to be an ugly modern building which had been a theological finishing school for nonconformist ministers. Whether it had been requisitioned for the Army or voluntarily vacated by the theologians I do not know, but some acrobatic wag among them had climbed to its roof and painted ICHABOD in large letters on a chimney stack and

24

this had been left as a memento. In moments of bitterness I
wondered whether the personnel of the place had changed
much, so gentlemanly, earnest and refined were its inhabitants
in 1940.

I walked through the gates alone, feeling some of the
shyness of a new boy entering a school, half expecting to be
asked by one of the old hands in khaki what my father did for a
living. I was in fact taken with a group of others fresh from
civilian life on a series of stops within the buildings to collect
items of dress, state personal details, draw bedding and be
allotted a place to sleep. All this was rather as I anticipated.
The battle-dress was in too short supply to guarantee a good
fit for all comers and I was lucky to obtain anything like one.
But I was not lucky at the boot store. The boots were all
secondhand—from casualties, someone suggested eerily—and
not always in pairs. Those I got were torture and I had to wear
them for a week until I could get into Winchester and buy
myself a pair of sturdy boots from Freeman, Hardy & Willis.
The bedding consisted of sacking filled with straw which we
collected like the children of Israel trying to make bricks, and
these were laid on the linoleum floor of the theologians' classrooms.

I was not worried by any of these minor privations for I had
expected life in the army to be rough and I had, after all, been
sleeping on the ground in a gypsy tent. What worried me that
day, and increasingly in the weeks that followed, was the
realization that my lot was not cast among men who matched
these conditions, the 'rapacious and licentious soldiery' I
expected to find blasphemously grumbling over them, but
among a collection of bourgeois intellectuals, schoolmasters,
graduates, bank-clerks, professional misfits, unsuccessful
actors and journalists, tourists' couriers and the like, the majority of them in their thirties or early forties. They did not
rebelliously blast their conditions but had one over-riding
grumble, that they were in the ranks at all and had not, as each
considered his case merited, been commissioned. What they

suffered, they thought, was all very well for ordinary soldiers who should expect such treatment; they ought to have been officers.

I am generalizing, of course. There were plenty of bright spirits among them as I came to see in time, but the first impression was for me a disillusionment. Their humour was of the teachers' common-room, little tee-hee jokes in French or funny rhymes, though they giggled obsequiously at the blundering banter of the NCOs training them. They were—again a generalization—too clever to be stirred by the idea behind their training, the forlorn hope of preparing a British force to combat German Intelligence. There was scarcely one of them who would not have moved to another branch of the Army if it meant a commission. They were mostly married men who even after being docked of separation allowance stinted themselves to help maintain their homes—praiseworthy, of course, but scarcely conducive to the rumbustious comradeship of the traditional soldier.

Moreover as I soon found, the whole place was humming with intrigue and invidiousness. On the very first night in the canteen I heard 'the Course at Matlock' mentioned with awe and longing. It appeared that as would-be Field Security men we underwent only preliminary training at Winchester and when considered ready were sent to Matlock in Derbyshire to take another course from which we would learn secret methods of resisting enemy espionage, sabotage and propaganda. Matlock, therefore, provided the only means of starting the real work to which we were supposed to be dedicated, for after clearing that hurdle we were returned to Winchester to be given a stripe and sent out 'on Section'. If a man passed the test of Winchester but failed that of Matlock his fate was considered a dire one. If he had come from an infantry unit he was returned to it as a failure, and hoary sergeants would make jokes like 'No wonder they wouldn't have you in the Intelligence Corps!' If on the other hand he failed after being a 'direct intake' at Winchester, and had come there straight from civilian life, he could not be sent to an infantry unit and his future was far more harrowing, for he was kept at Winchester in some capacity at the FS Training Centre, in charge of the boot store, clothing store or cookhouse fatigues, as corporal in charge of sanitation, medical orderly or company clerk. So about the premises were unfortunate individuals known to have 'failed the Course', held up to entrants as Awful Examples of those who had lacked keenness or in some way neglected to charm the instructors at Matlock.

This gave a certain urgency to men's efforts to learn the elements of military training, and a good deal of care was taken not to antagonize the NCO instructors, or to be in any direction out of line. Trainees might have been the students of the former King Alfred's College for the correctness of their conduct and the piety of the sentiments they expressed.

The officers were remote. They lived in the private portion of the buildings and it was a fortnight before I knew them by sight and only after a month or two was I on speaking terms with any of them. But the NCOs were far from remote, they were everywhere, all the time. They were of one derivation—they were Guardsmen who after serving their time had joined the Police and had now been called up to be given three stripes or a crown and told to inculcate the principles of peacetime soldiering into the wayward recruits of the Intelligence Corps. I was told that none of them, while in the Guards, had risen above the rank of lance-corporal, or in the Police of police constable, and that this was their first attempt at giving orders to others. I must say that they did not make a bad job of it and strident military voices rang daylong through the grounds and cloisters. This made the kind of bedlam that I suppose most recruits in the army faced in those days, the wrathful bellowing of NCOs, the self-conscious aloofness of officers, desperate preparations for kit inspection, the grim exertions of physical training, hurried dressing and pungent meals, attempts to manipulate weapons, even lifelike bayonet charges. In our case it was all given a grotesque irony by the fact that we were trained in what had been a place dedicated to the orderly study of mild theology.

The NCOs were not bad fellows; indeed as I came to know in time, several of them were human and their task, to make a soldier out of a semi-intellectual civilian in a few weeks, was a well-nigh impossible one. They shouted and cursed and threatened as they had been shouted at when they first joined the Guards. In the eyes of recruits they were Terrors.

Small wonder, considering the whole set-up, that there was a sickening predominance of 'keen men' among the trainees, keen not only to learn drill and musketry but to pander to the whims of their instructors. Small wonder that they watched one another with invidious fear of success in a rival, that they spoke with head-shaking of a rebellious act, ('That will never get him to Matlock!'), or that they curried favour with those on whom their future seemed to depend.

This was not what I had looked forward to or desired. I suppose—to be honest—that I expected my fellow soldiers to be much like the men I had played darts with every night in country pubs, or the hard cases I met round the circus, or the pea-pickers or hop-pickers, or down-and-outs in London, or indeed any roughish unintellectual crowd with whom I knew I could get on. I should have been warned by the fact that the main qualification for FS candidates was that they spoke at least one foreign language. It was calculated that forty per cent of the personnel training at that time had been schoolmasters in civil life. Excellent fellows, of course, among whom I had earned my living for five years as a boy, but a disappointment of the absurdly romantic hopes with which I had joined the Army as a private. I determined to get through Winchester training as quickly as possible.

[2]

At first it seemed that I should succeed. There had been a

balls-up—and how familiar *that* term was to become—either at Matlock or at Winchester and it was now realized that at the end of the next fortnight no trained men would be ready to 'go on the Course'. There was only one remedy. The new intake, my own, must be rushed through their training in two weeks, concentrating into that time all the instruction that would normally take six. Since there were too many of us to be accommodated at Matlock, a selection had to be made and those who had been through an OTC were chosen. This was the only time when those boring hours in boyhood of drill and route marches were of any service to me.

A sergeant—late of the Scots Guards—took the chosen few in hand and explained how lucky we were. We should be worked to death, have not a minute to ourselves for two weeks, undergo instruction in drill, physical training, motor cycling, weapon-training, map-reading, saluting, something called Intelligence and Unarmed Combat all within fourteen days. It would be gruelling and exhausting, *but* we should be out of Winchester in a flash and away to the paradise of life 'on Section' sooner than anyone who had come through the depot.

He did not exaggerate. It was a back-breaking experience for us and doubtless for big Sergeant Sprott who mothered us through it. But at the end of it he told us that we had 'all passed' and should leave for Matlock next day.

Then came one of those blows which have punctuated my life and which I have come to recognize now as devastating at the time but seen in retrospect the greatest good fortune.

"Cuke," said Sergeant Sprott with his Glaswegian enunciation. "You're not going to Matlock tomorrow. There's *something wrong with your papers*."

Next to failing the course, having 'something wrong with one's papers' was the most dismal circumstance that could befall a Field Security trainee. It meant a long wait at the depot, or even permanent consignment to the staff with the Course failures. It implied that one had not oneself passed the Security test that cleared one for receiving instruction in

Security. Nothing whatever could be done about it till some mysterious body at MI headquarters decided on one's case. There were a number of unfortunates at Winchester who had 'something wrong with their papers', and so could go no further, men who had fought on the Republican side in Spain and so were Reds, men who had belonged to Mosley's or some Anglo-German friendship organization and so were Nazis. But I was neither, and puzzled myself for weeks about it.

Information came only after I had been cleared of suspicion and sent to Matlock at last. It was a complete surprise to me. I imagined several explanations—that MI knew that I had once lunched with Admiral Sir Barry Domville who had proudly shown me a telegram from Goering, or that I had been in Germany in 1938 and had friends there, or that I had spoken at a Foyle's luncheon on the Press and Germany. But it was none of these. A clearance certificate from the police in the place of his attestment was demanded for every recruit to Field Security and the Inspector or Superintendent at Pershore had stated that he knew nothing about me except that I had spent the summer there *living with gypsies*. A highly suspicious circumstance, MI had considered, until that autumn when my gypsy novel *Glorious* appeared. "Oh, he's a writer. He was studying gypsies for a book. *That's* all right!" decided MI, and I was cleared.

This piece of comedy, characteristic of the War Office, was enacted some months later, and after repeated requests from Winchester for a decision. For the moment I 'had something wrong with my papers' and could not go on the mysterious Course at Matlock.

Everyone was sympathetic about this. "Hard luck, old man," said the schoolmasters with whom I had drilled and sweated. They marched off to the station singing.

[3]

The next fortnight was probably the worst, speaking in terms of hard or cushy times, that I passed in the army.

The trainees at the Winchester depot were divided into two mobs, lots or showers, 'A' Company under CSM Dixon and 'B' Company under CSM Drakely. They were both good soldiers and instructors trying to maintain their standards as ex-Guardsmen rather than ex-policemen, Dixon less vociferously than Drakely who was something of a martinet. I had been in Dixon's Company and when he heard that I was being 'held back because of papers' he commiserated and said, "Anyhow you're finished with all this square-bashing. You'll be given a job with the depot police until we can get you to Matlock." He then went off to Matlock in charge of his Company and would not return for a fortnight.

Meanwhile I came under Drakely and hearing that I had been promised this job—the best number in the depot—he sent for me and spent five explosive minutes destroying any such pretensions. Perhaps he remembered similar bollockings when he had first joined the Guards, or perhaps he was put out by Dixon's friendly concessions. He said all that an incensed sergeant-major could say, maintaining his reputation for giving hell to all trainees whom he regarded as half-witted scroungers not fit to wear the King's uniform. It was a most effective display and to back it up he put me on cookhouse fatigues for five days running, an unheard-of penalty.

I recall these battles long ago, since few men who have served in the ranks can have escaped similar episodes at some time and most will recognize the sensations. Drakely became a good friend later, as I shall recount, but faced with five days of peeling spuds and washing dishes I would cheerfully have shot him in the back if we had gone into action. That fatigue, the only one I did in the army, was made more bearable by the variety of men who shared it of whom I remember Lou Preager, a BBC danceband leader famous at the time, Stephen Haggard, an actor and writer who was killed in North Africa later, and a little Welsh minister whose puckish humour and quaint appearance kept us all sane and even cheerful. Potato-peeling was done with rusty knives instead of peelers under a lance-corporal who was one of the depot's oddities, since he had 'failed the Course' and been given the post in recompense. As day after day I saw my name on Part II orders under Cookhouse Fatigue I began to wonder whether I should ever do anything else in the army but peel potatoes and wash dishes.

But deliverance came from a lucky recollection by a certain staff sergeant in the Company office, Harry Payne, who had read a book of mine and secured my transfer to the Regimental Police.

[4]

At that time I found only one man I had known in civilian life, Charles Fisher, a name I see occasionally in the index of one of the many books about Dylan Thomas.

I had met him at a pub in the Cotswolds. As a friend of poets and a would-be poet himself, he was on what he would have shuddered to call a walking-tour. He was then a boy of nineteen, rather goodlooking with large deep-blue eyes and a pleasantly resonant speaking voice, free—or I rather think freed—of a Welsh intonation and vocabulary. He was from Swansea and told me very soon that he was one of the Kardomah Café circle of Dylan's friends. He was not affected, yet he cultivated amusing affectations, calling himself Carl instead of Charles, wearing an angler's tweed hat spiked with ornamental flies, carrying a heavy cudgel and walking about the countryside a poet-at-large on money he had saved from his pay as a clerk.

He had genuine enthusiasms for literary figures as well as for their work. I remember him telling me that Dylan was the greatest poet since Shelley and that he considered it his duty to stand up when Dylan came into a room in recognition of this. He thought John Cowper Powys's *Glastonbury Romance* one of the greatest novels in the English language—books and writers being to him either great or worthless and no nonsense about

it. He stayed in my Cotswold cottage for some days and I
remember trying in vain to impress him with the fact that I was
a professional writer, a qualification which had no meaning for
him. I did not write poetry like Dylan's and so was damned.
"Que diable allait-il faire dans cette galère?" I asked when I
found him quietly at home among the trainees at the FS depot,
but he at once lifted me out of the depression induced by five
days in the cookhouse. He had a humorously fatalistic attitude
to our surroundings, an eye for the oddities of training and a
sense of proportion unimpaired by uniform. We went for a
long walk through the Hampshire countryside, and returning
to tea in a Winchester café were rewarded by the sight of Dr
Negrín, the refugee Prime Minister of Republican Spain,
having tea at the next table. I had recently translated *The Last
Days of Madrid* by Colonel Casado and felt something like
contempt for Negrín, whose conduct was neither courageous
nor honest, but the Spanish Civil War seemed a long time past.

After that Sunday afternoon in which I had been so encouraged and amused by Charles Fisher, I began to settle down
at the depot, realizing that there could be many fates worse
than mine of being 'held back' in Winchester where life was
full of comedy and duties were not heavy and this coarse and
ugly uniform could be lightly worn.

[5]

What seems most strange in retrospect about that autumn
was how in joining the Army I had escaped the war, how in
settling my own affairs with the State I had ceased to feel much
concern for its dangers. The Battle of Britain was at its fearful
climax but although two of my friends had already been killed
in it and I tried to feel its horror, it had little reality for me
beyond the posters of the newspapermen which imitated
cricket scoreboards, Theirs 78 Ours 17. A few months ago I

had read my daily paper with wholehearted concern and apprehension, had fumed over Narvik and the fall of Belgium and France and felt one of a beleagured population, but now I found the affairs of the depot concerned me far more closely.

That was the great compensation for all the petty sacrifices—of freedom, of prosperity, of comfort—in Army life. I did not worry any more. I began, in my childishly optimistic way, to make the best of my circumstances and found them full of possibilities.

This was another common experience, I think, this sense of having entered a strange world in which the old values counted for nothing. It was like passing through the looking-glass or down the rabbit-hole for Alice, and though one sought as she did for some logic or sense of proportion, one had to conclude that although these had to exist one would never find them by the standards of civilian life. Things that would have seemed trivial took on vast importance, and important things, like the course of the war, one's own rough system of ethics, pre-war relationships and ambitions faded to insignificance. A kit parade was more momentous than a public appearance, failure to 'pass' something or other was as tragic as the death of a friend. In this half-world of little events the happenings that had once been real and fateful were forgotten and one lived wholly for the military day. The writing of books, the little successes of my profession, the travels and adventures I had achieved, were scarcely a memory. I lived for the small compensations of soldiering, and I was perfectly content. I felt a little of what must be the supreme reward of the monastic life, an indifference to affairs beyond it, a day-to-day satisfaction with a less mundane philosophy.

And yet in sense, and in its details, more mundane. To thrive on a few encouraging words from an unthinking oaf in authority, to delight in a cup of bad tea and a cigarette snatched between parades, to laugh inordinately at clumsy humour or be moved almost to tears by another's misfortunes—these were not the natural preoccupations of a mature and fairly exper-

ienced man, yet in all those years of army life they were mine.
I was wholly lost in that life, following it with all I had of
capacity to experience. For six years I scarcely wrote a word or
read a book and when it was over I came to the surface like a
blinded pit pony. Friends who had followed the historic events
of those six years found me unintelligent about the war that
was over and uncomprehending of the changes in public life.
I had been in the Army.

[6]

To return to the FS Training Centre at Winchester which
just then was my whole existence.

Neither the duties nor the authority of the depot police,
somewhat grandly called the RP or regimental police, were
ever closely defined. There were about ten of us and we wore
impressive armbands and carried batons when on duty.
Because everyone in the Army has to have charge of something,
even if it is no more than his own kit, we were in charge of the
'police post', a desk inside the main entrance, and had to 'check
in' all those entering, even if they had only been on an hour's
exit permit to the town. Lock-up, for which there was some
military term, was at ten o'clock and flustered stragglers would
hurry in at 10.5, begging that their entry in the book should be
entered as 9.55 to avoid penalties for the frightful offence of
being a few minutes late, in which conspiracy we always
joined. Such was the spell cast by words like 'passing the
Course' and 'getting to Matlock' that seasoned captains of
commerce who had commanded scores of employees, or men
prominent in the arts would come rushing in out of breath and
swearing that the clock at the police post was fast or vehemently
asking us to perjure ourselves.

Besides 'checking in' we had night duty several times a week
and strolled about the grounds or round the outbuildings

looking for intruders. I never found one and do not know what
I should have done if I had. On these nights we were permitted
to raid the cookhouse for food and frequently found sausages,
eggs and bacon concealed by the cooks for their own susten-
ance. Sometimes there were air-raids on Southampton, eighteen
miles away, but the Germans evidently did not think the
training centre for defensive intelligence worth a bomb.

A Frenchman from Madagascar named Seneque shared this
night-duty with me on several occasions. He had a gift for
Gallic small talk and we passed the hours pleasantly enough.

After the first week or two I never ate in the dining-room
for I found the rancid smell of long-ago meals nauseating and
the enamel plates only half clean, while the food though not
uneatable was dreary. I would go without breakfast till the
morning break when hot buns and rolls from a shop in the
town were sold in the canteen with coffee made from bottled
essence. After that I waited till tea-time, since the Winchester
cafés still sold poached eggs or soft roes or baked beans on
toast. At night, while some money remained to me, I dined at
the Southgate with Eddie Bates.

He was a Course failure, a pretty-faced young man whom I
had known long ago, also in the Cotswolds. He was the son of
the millionaire shipowner Sir Percy Bates and was the gentlest
and most likeable soul at the depot, without any sign of a chip
on his shoulder though his failure of the Course was a spiteful
injustice by the ladylike instructors at Matlock. Eddie had not
sought to improve his position in the depot, had in fact
volunteered to be orderly in the Sergeants' Mess, a situation
that would have seemed humiliating to anyone else. He was
given a large allowance by his father and had an experienced
taste in wine, and we dined rather splendidly. The Southgate
then had a very fair cellar and we dallied with the Wine List to
our great enjoyment and wellbeing, unconscious of our
uniforms and of the irritations of the past day.

Eddie's story thereafter was a brief and tragic one. He was
transferred to the RAF, qualified as a pilot and was killed

before the end of 1941. His father refused to believe he was
dead and left a will which caused much confusion since his
property was to be held in trust for his son until some time
after the end of hostilities in the hope that Eddie was even then
alive.

[7]

I became almost as much an old inhabitant as the permanent
staff. I came to know the officers, the Adjutant, Captain Sutherland, Major Wilkinson, the officer in charge of posting (a useful
contact if I should ever get through Matlock), Captain Lord
Northesk, a cheery little man who looked older than he was,
and Peter Lawless, my own Company Commander, a beefy
character who had been an international rugger player and the
rugger correspondent of the *Daily Telegraph*. (He was killed
later in the war.) Sutherland came to depot dances every
Saturday and we used to remain at the bar drinking beer and
talking till long after the gymnasium was empty and the corporal in charge of the canteen was yawning. I liked this man
who could be—in army terms—a bastard in military matters
but loved to talk long over a pint and had no snobbery about
rank when not on parade.

I was asked to edit the depot magazine. It was called *HUSH!
An I.C.D. Erratic Sporting and Dramatic* and was produced by
Roneo on folio sheets. It was pitifully like all magazines of its
sort, which in turn resemble school magazines, being full of
sporting results, jokes of strictly local appeal, parodies of
Kipling, accounts of concerts.

[8]

Life in fact became a sort of parody of life in a preparatory school, with new boys arriving, 'frightful rows' going on, football matches against rival establishments, favouritism, whispered confidences, and if not tuck-boxes at least pocket-money to spend in the canteen. Instead of school walks we had motor-cycling under instruction, instead of end-of-term examinations we had tests, instead of popular or unpopular masters we had sergeant instructors, instead of a Head we had the Commandant, and we did PT, wrote letters home, grumbled at the food, quarrelled among ourselves and tried to pass the Common Entrance Examination to go to Matlock.

I even had a 'visit from my people' for my youngest brother, already a captain, walked into the officers' Mess and asked my Company Commander for permission to 'take me out to lunch' which was given, the request being considered in no way abnormal as one between grown men training for war. Moreover I was asked to tea by the Commandant's wife, a charming woman who guessed what it would mean to a man living in barracks to sit in a fireside armchair and eat thin bread and butter.

Incidents of that kind multiplied during my months at Winchester. Among old Army papers I find on the back of a menu card the following, which was written by Lord Tennyson, then serving in the Rifle Brigade whose depot was near ours at Winchester, to Lord Northesk, of our own staff. '*Dear David, Pte R. C. Cooke will be late reporting to barracks tonight as he cannot get a taxi, and has been helping Phyllis get her car out of the car park which has stuck in the mud. Love to Betty. Lionel.*' The date of this curiosity was during the Battle of Britain, but does it argue anything except that the English have their own way of making war?

Concerts were a weekly event and Stephen Haggard produced a one-act play of mine called *Banquo's Chair*. Motor cycling was, and remained throughout my service, a relaxation, indeed a positive pleasure, and the hill-climbing test was fun. I was completely absorbed in the contrasts and absurdities of depot life and though I wanted to move on to something less parochial I was quite happy, supported by a self-righteous belief that in joining the army I had at least tried to be useful. I had no personal ambition. A lance-corporal 'on Section' was as high as my sights were set.

[9]

Sergeant-Major Drakely, the Terror of the depot, who had once given me that magnificent rocket, was appeased by a darts match between the warrant officers and other ranks which I organized. I would have liked to make it between trainees and staff but not enough of our scholarly personnel played the plebeian game. In the first round I was matched against Drakely and fortunately lost, which enabled him to say that he had defeated the author of the only book on the game, and thereafter he was my friend.

But I attracted other hostilities among my fellow trainees for in the Army, even more than in life, there are always men outraged by the sight of small privileges or comforts which by ingenuity the self-indulgent are able to attain, even if these do not affect them. Contrivance or wangling, admittedly not an admirable faculty, was *mal vu* by the intellectuals suffering the frustration of Winchester, and who could blame them? But it came naturally to me and was really little more than a determination to enjoy whatever circumstances I found. My long period of being 'held back' had made me a familiar figure in the depot and to the authorities an odd and harmless one. I slept longer and ate better and had more freedom than most and of course it rankled.

I was particularly disliked by those who, instead of coming to FS direct from civilian life as I had done, were sent first for five or six months to the oppressive discipline of an Infantry Training Centre. They were disillusioned when they came to

Winchester at last and found not a cabalistic society of counter-spies but a collection of men undergoing military training by ex-guardsmen and realized that they had it all to do again.

Among these was one little coterie of smart soldiers, younger than most and far, far keener. They all belonged to the body then called the Oxford Group movement, having been converted by one of their number perhaps as a relief from the rigours of infantry training.

"*We* think," this man told me when I commiserated with him on those wasted months, "that the ITC was a very good thing for us. It taught us to obey orders."

I found this funny and said so.

"It's all very well for you to hang about the depot, drinking too much and thinking of nothing but a good time. You don't seem to realize *there's a war on!*"

This was true enough. But when they asked me to join one of their meetings, I revolted.

"I'm a Catholic," I said.

"That doesn't matter! Lots of our chaps were Roman Catholics *at first*. We don't object, whatever you may have been."

Hopeless to argue. It was their bloody complacency that riled me. They looked on me as a lost sheep, which by their standards I was, and shook their heads in sorrow when I managed to escape a route march or fatigue.

Not all the men who had suffered from too much spit and polish both in the ITC and here were as submissive as they were —some were genuinely angry at the waste of time and wanted in a phrase of the period to 'get on with the job'. I remember, for instance, the journalist R. W. Thompson who later wrote a perceptive book about that over-rated soldier Montgomery, fuming about the delay when he sojourned in the depot for a short time. During the next four or five years, while the majority of the army could do nothing but train for the far-off goal of the Normandy landings, many of them almost lost heart. If we could have foreseen that long period of military preparation, the training at the Field Security depot would itself have seemed more logical.

To other units training in the district, we were little better than the military police. (Field Security had in fact been started as the FS Wing of the CMP.) We were believed to have luxurious headquarters and to spend pleasant days being lectured on spycraft, or motor cycling about the countryside. A detachment of the East Surreys was under canvas near by and came to use our showerbaths on several afternoons a week. One of my RP duties was to induce them to remove their boots before crossing the polished floor of the gymnasium.

"What, and walk about in my stockinged feet?" one asked indignantly. "What do you take us for? Mohammedans? This isn't a training centre, it's a bleeding Mosque."

It was called other things by the Army I had wanted to join, and Field Security personnel were considered more dangerous than the spies they were popularly supposed to catch, snooping, making trouble, lecturing bored troops, carrying out security tests and generally being a nuisance. When I remember those months in the one-time theological college I can only think what a futile collection we were to be matched against the ruthless Intelligence men of Germany. Yet I do not see how the basic idea behind Field Security could in the circumstances have been much better.

To take a number of men able to speak foreign languages, to train them as soldiers to a degree when they would be recognized as such both by other units and by the enemy, to teach them what could be taught of ways to combat enemy espionage, sabotage and propaganda, to send them out in small Sections, one officer, one sergeant-major, two sergeants and eight lance-corporals to be attached to an infantry or other unit, with specific duties both in training and action, was not a foolish scheme and might have been a very useful one. It was crippled by the fact that linguists in England (at that time, anyway) belonged for the most part to one section of society, and were not the best men for the very tough work necessary.

No worthwhile instruction could be given about their probable duties, and Sections lacked authority and were nearly all
commanded by officers drawn from other branches and warrant
officers appointed for their proficiency in bumph and discipline
who had little or no interest in Security work. Moreover, the
English character did not, on the whole, lend itself to this kind
of activity. Finally, though a high degree of qualification was
demanded there was little or no advancement possible for
Field Security NCOs who saw their officers brought in from
elsewhere. Logically these NCOs should have been ruthless,
physically tough, able to mix with all ranks and to endure the
hardest conditions, filled with hatred of the enemy and suspicion of civilians; in fact they were gentlemanly, restrained and
thoughtful men, too humane for modern warfare, too concerned with family life to let themselves go in the bestial business
they had to face. But that could be said of most conscript
soldiers of all armies. They just were not bad enough.

[10]

I had been at the depot for three months before I made a
friend in any but the casual sense in which fellow trainees are
all friends, and when I did so the relationship was an in-
congruous one. Julyan Pickering was the son of the Mayor of a
London borough, a short, husky man, humorous and even-
tempered, ten years younger than I was. What was more to the
point, in the artificial circumstances in which we lived, he had
the rank of bombadier, having left the Royal Artillery for this
venture. He regretted doing so, not because it meant his losing
a stripe but because his naturally rebellious nature was offended
by the prim and fawning behaviour of trainees. We had in
common a latent and controlled anarchism, a liking for public
bars and unrefined conversation, and a sense of the ridiculous
which made entertainment out of the incongruities of depot
life.

Friendship is almost a necessity in the ranks; everyone needs someone to lie for him, look after his kit in a crisis, drink with him in leisure hours, lend him money, help him to pass some footling test, hear his complaints and keep him sane when the whole thing seems to be out of hand. Army friendships are of a substance wholly different from those of civilian life and rarely outlast the conditions in which they are formed. Julyan and I were inseparable for a month or two and contrived to meet in several places after we had left the depot.

It made that Christmas of 1940 a more bearable occasion.

CHAPTER THREE

Matlock and After

[1]

I THOUGHT at that time that the war was notable for the frequency with which those in command were suddenly relieved of their posts. It started with the War Minister himself, Leslie Hore-Belisha, who was followed by Ironside and several lesser but still mighty figures. Sometimes this was due to incompetence or what seemed it, sometimes to the fact that a rival was thought to have better claims, and sometimes to jealousy or intrigue among the military high-ups.

Soon after Christmas it befell our Commandant, Lieutenant-Colonel F. C. Davies MC, but this was a shameful case of nepotism in reverse.

Field Security may not have been a thunderously successful arm of the forces but it certainly did useful work and, such as it was, it owed a great deal to Davies. Since I have described the Training Centre as a sort of school I would say he was the founder, for in its early days as a branch of the CMP at Aldershot he was put in command and helped to raise it to an independent body. He was a dry, self-contained man, something of an idealist and something of a martinet. Doubtless he was fairly unpopular at the War Office and doubtless this enabled the civilian power which tumbled him to achieve a very mean objective. He lost his command and colonelcy but the FS training centre lost a very able enthusiast and never quite recovered from it.

For me, however, this event was dwarfed in importance by a dramatic turn in my own affairs for I was suddenly informed that at toe end of the week I should leave for Matlock to 'take

44

the Course' not, as one might have thought, of therapeutic baths but of instruction in Defensive Intelligence.

Before leaving I received a great deal of advice from my friends who had passed or failed this Course and knew its pitfalls. I could not have been blamed if I had misunderstood the whole tenor of this advice since most of it appertained to dress and appearance.

"You must show you're the Right Type. Personality is most important. Make sure you have decently fitting battle-dress and a presentable pair of boots."

"What for?"

"The morning parade. And don't speak more than you can help. Let the instructors do the talking. It's the quiet type who gets through. Don't forget to have a haircut before you go. A neat short haircut goes a long way."

"Don't I have to learn anything?"

"Oh yes, but the most important thing is personality. I shouldn't leave the headquarters, if I were you. It's not forbidden to go out for a drink but it doesn't give the best impression. And don't laugh. When you're on the Course, I mean."

"Not?"

"Definitely not, unless one of the instructors makes a joke. Laughter is not encouraged. Is that the smartest forage cap you can find? You'll never get good marks on the morning inspection with that."

A corporal named Stirrup, known as Tiffy Stirrup, was the best hand in the depot at 'boning' a pair of boots, a work of many hours in which, with the aid of spittle and certain secret ingredients, the leather of Army boots could be given a spurious sheen and look like patent leather. He did a pair for me and advised me to purchase two clean dusters in which they were to be enfolded separately, to be brought out and used only for the daily inspection. I had a suit of battle-dress made by a local tailor, a most elegant piece of work in the smoothest serge. With these accoutrements and a brilliantly polished hat badge in a new forage cap I set off with a Company of trainees to receive the momentous instruction and if possible pass the test of suitability for the work I had—long ago it seemed—chosen.

[2]

If training at Winchester had been disappointingly full of para-military nonsense, that at Matlock was plain farce and an insult to even the mildly intelligent. Small wonder that laughter was not encouraged—it would have overcome all but the keenest and most dutiful among us.

The largest hotel in the Derbyshire spa had been requisitioned for the purpose of an Intelligence school and its lounges and dining rooms were occupied by officers receiving instruction on one or another aspect of the work. The former staff quarters housed the eighty-odd FS men who were undergoing their training Course.

On our arrival at the Hydro the instructors appeared, and it did not take much perception or experience to see that most of them were queers. No one has a greater admiration than I for the brazen invert, in the Army or out of it, or a stronger wish to identify myself with his resistance to conformity. In the last war he showed himself brave and resourceful and kept his cheerfulness and wit under the most intolerable conditions, including those of the war in Burma. But in the uniform of a sergeant-major, trusted to decide which of the men under instruction were fit for certain onerous duties, he was not at his best.

That first evening we were allotted to particular instructors for the Course, or rather picked by them like a football side at school. 'I'll have him, with the big drum," said the Salvation Army convert when told he could choose a hymn in the smoking-room story, and it was all rather like that.

Next morning we went on parade, that parade famous in far-off Winchester for its spit and polish. Now, in 1970, as I write this in the library of a Cypriot monastery, I wonder whether I can make it credible to a reader of two generations later.

The officer commanding the FS Wing at Matlock took the parade, but there was no drill, no movement even, only a display of men standing smartly to attention in prettified uniform. The OC passed along the lines and congratulated the instructors on the turn-out of the men under them, or spoke more in sorrow than in anger of a stain on the webbing of gaiters, an unglazed boot, or the lack of a razor-sharp crease in the battle-dress trousers. Good marks were given to those whose appearances were faultless and there were hard words for careless men with unteutonic haircuts.

"Here's a smart turn-out, Sergeant-Major," one would overhear. "But I see the jacket of his battle-dress is not buttoned on to the trousers at one point. Yes, there's a button missing there. Pity that. He might have qualified for a Mention."

There was an element of tragedy in this, for the button might cost that unfortunate man his whole FS career and send him back to Winchester to clean wash-houses for the rest of the war.

We became aware, too, of the extraordinary contortions of our instructors, lifting their legs knee high to stamp, not in petulance but in a musical-comedy imitation of Guardsmen on sentry-go. Unexpectedly deep voices came out of their lungs and their faces were sternly set in rehearsed lines. They were pictures.

After parade a short break was allowed so that we could remove our parade boots and titivated uniforms and put them away until tomorrow. We then came to the classrooms more naturally dressed. This happened each day during the two weeks of that Course and there was time, our instructor solemnly told us, for a man who had not distinguished himself in the first few parades to make retribution before the end of the Course.

[3]

On the first morning, before we received any instruction, there was an impressive little ceremony when each man had to sign an undertaking that he would never reveal what he was about to learn. (My name by chance was omitted from the roll so that I never gave the undertaking.) This was promising and we were all a-gog as they say, to hear the deepest secrets of I(b).

Each instructor lectured from a set précis, as might be expected, and left time for questions. It was now that the trainee had a chance to shine, to show that he had intelligently followed the lecture, that he was interested, that he was the Right Type. The lectures, however, told us nothing that any reasonably responsible man did not know already and the whole thing, supposed to be security instruction, guidance in enemy methods, teaching of experience already gained, was a hotch-potch of clichés about espionage, sabotage and propaganda delivered with solemnity in the artificially refined accents of the instructors. We had come half across England to hear this. Was our journey, we asked ourselves in a catch-phrase of the time, really necessary?

Anything could change from one day to another in that citizen army and it may well be that I hit a bad patch at Matlock and that earlier or later Courses were better served but early in 1941 it was all unbelievably silly. The RSM, an intelligent soldier and the only one of the warrant officers to have come out of France at the time of Dunkirk, had put in for a transfer and the rest of the instructors were in a tizzy about who would take his place. They would visit one another's classrooms during lectures with the latest news and whispered confidences could be overheard by the trainees—'I heard the CO say . . .' or 'I believe it has all been decided . . .'.

As the Course went on some curious characteristics came to light among us. Men trying to give the impression of being the Right Type and finding that there was so much at stake, no longer cared what their fellows thought of their behaviour and went all out for the approval of the instructors. One went too far—a big sentimental creature with a large moustache, he said in answer to a question on sabotage, "I love this old country, every stick and stone of her," and promptly failed the Course. He wasn't trying for effect; he talked like that all the time. Others depended, as I did, on keeping quiet and looking interested, a meaner form of hypocrisy perhaps.

Half way through the Course I could stand it no longer and abandoned hope of passing. If this was Field Security I might just as well stay at Winchester and would probably be more useful there. In any case it was dangerous to do too well for it could mean being recommended for a commission and being sent to an OCTU to become an infantry subaltern. One good-looking youngster, quite inarticulate but physically splendid, was recommended by the instructors to join them on the Matlock staff and did so to their great satisfaction.

I no longer took the safe way of nonentity. Sunday morning was dedicated to fatigues, classroom cleaning and whatnot, and trainees showed their keenness to scrub floors, unless they obtained leave to attend church in the town. This was so frowned-on that men who had put themselves down as 'C of E' were automatically refused by the NCO on duty. But I was aware of a curious belief in the Army that Roman Catholics had some mysterious sincerity and compulsion in matters of religion lacking in other denominations. I asked in a conspiratorial voice for leave to 'attend Mass', and the instructor, looking as though he expected the Pope himself to curse him with bell, book and candle if he refused, gave a stealthy nod. This might well have cost me my chances of passing the Course, but I was past caring.

There was a pub opposite the Hydro. It was not absolutely forbidden to us but, according to popular belief, it was Watched. I took to 'dropping in for a quick one' when there was a chance and felt that I had still further alienated myself from the righteous. Worse still, I began to take an interest in the sur-

D

roundings outside the headquarters. I found Matlock had the melancholy of all the inland spas I knew, Tunbridge Wells, Cheltenham, Malvern, Bath or Spa itself which in spite of the beauty of the Ardennes seems permanently under a cloud, or Aix-les-Bains, even more beautiful and sad. I met other servicemen in bars, Norman Trace whom I had not met since we were partners in an antique business in Gloucestershire and a RNAS pilot who told me quietly on a rocky walk outside the town that he did not expect to survive the war—very few of his crowd did. I began, in other words, to escape the rigours of the Course and enjoy myself and was astounded on the last day to hear that I had passed, with no distinction at all but sufficiently well to return to Winchester and await being 'sent out on Section'.

[4]

The fatuity of Matlock was particularly hard to take at this time, January 1941, because just then the English, as far as it was ever possible to them, were taking the war seriously. Invasion still threatened and there was no more talk, as there had been in the first months of war, of playing at soldiers. A Home Guard was enlisted and road blocks built to prepare for landings. The 'island fortress' as a phrase was not yet used; it came into the vocabulary of civilians only when it could safely romanticize the past, but there were serious efforts to make it more than an idea.

In the Army there was a fashion for invasion exercises in which an enemy force was supposed to have landed somewhere on the East Coast and troops in the area were disposed to meet them. The role of Field Security in these should have been a very active one, trained as we were supposed to be to deal with enemy activities most dangerous in such an invasion. But at this time we had only recently ceased to be the FSP and become the FS Wing of the Intelligence Corps and our powers were uncertain, our duties ill-defined and our personnel, as we have seen in my case, arbitrarily chosen and erratically trained. There was not much we could do.

Someone had the bright idea of sending men from the depot into the areas of invasion exercises to impersonate Enemy Agents, to see how much information they could gather about the defence. The attacking forces existed only in the imagination, like most else in these exercises, though they were real enough for the men who had to sweat and hump out-of-date weapons about.

So now, back at Winchester from that ridiculous Course at Matlock, promoted to lance-corporal as a fully qualified FS man, I was sent up to the Highlands to act as enemy agent in one of the largest of these Exercises, that of the Fifty-first Highland Division whose headquarters were at Aberlour, Morayshire.

My fellow-spy was Francis Noel-Baker, then a lance-corporal awaiting posting as I was. He had not long left his public school, a cold fish I thought, humourless but highly intelligent. Field Security seems to have left a mark on him, for after the war he wrote a book about a visit to Spain in which he imagined himself to be shadowed everywhere by Franco's agents. Later as Labour MP for Swindon he introduced and succeeded in getting on the Statute book a law against advertising cigarettes on television, one of those grandmotherly pieces of legislation for 'people's own good' which I find so detestable in spirit and intent. But just then he was a keen youngster with ice-blue eyes who took our role seriously and saw nothing comic in our two hyphenated names and contrasting ages and characters brought together for the nebulous purpose we served.

The whole thing was funny and enjoyable and it may have given some satisfaction to those who planned the defence to know that we were 'arrested' by the FS Section in the area, though not before we had made our discoveries and 'com-

municated' them to the symbolic headquarters of the non-
existent attacking force. Playing at soldiers indeed, but not
without a certain excitement within its own premise of
realism.

Among some old Army papers I have found the report I
wrote in the Grand Hotel, Elgin, at the end of that Exercise
thirty years ago. It is written by hand on the printed notepaper
of the hotel, and reads now like an ingenious attempt to cover
up our indiscretion in having confided to a civilian that we
were acting as bogus agents in the scheme, and that, as I
remember it, is what happened. How important it all seemed
then!

[5]

Back at Winchester I had barely time to find a comfortable
bunk (two-tiered wooden structures had been supplied by now),
and go to the Southgate with Julyan Pickering a few times, and
watch the Oxford Groupers march off on their way to an
infantry OCTU, before new schemes were under way with
which to occupy our time profitably. The depot was apparently
ahead of schedule with eighty or so trained men, for whom no
sections had yet been formed, kicking their heels at Winchester,
and someone decided to put them into provisional Sections
and send them here and there, whenever accommodation
could be found. It did not take much contrivance to get myself
into one of these with two friends, Julyan Pickering and a
charming, inconsequently romantic, humorous character,
amusingly named Morley-Mower.

I dislike the use of four-letter words in writing, not on
moral but on aesthetical grounds. They look ugly and rather
silly in a page of print and no one, certainly not D. H. Lawrence, has even been able to use them without an air of bravado.
For the most obvious and functional of them I still insist,

against the advice of publishers and critics, on the use of a
- - - -, with or without -ing after it. But there is one of them
which cannot be paraphrased in discussing Army relationships
—the no less ugly but essential word shit, applied, only half
metaphorically, to certain types happily not common. In
civilian life it is a boomerang word and denotes the speaker as
often as the nominee, but in the Army everyone knows what a
shit is. Each of us might have his own opinion of what makes a
bore, a bully, a bootlicker, a sponger or a braggart, but a shit,
compounded of most of these, is a creature recognizable to all.
Now the three of us found that we had one as the Sergeant of
our provisional section.

He was a short officious man who had been promoted in an
infantry regiment for work in the orderly room. In a flat,
persistently aggressive voice, loud enough to catch the attention of passing officers, he shouted unnecessary orders. He
toadied to those above him and harassed those below. Besides,
he looked a shit. One had only to see that undersized, irritable,
bustling man to know what one was up against.

Perhaps the action we took will show that we knew little
and cared less for Army tradition—certainly we should have
been sent to the Glasshouse in the peacetime Army. We were
determined not to leave the depot, even on this temporary
assignment, with *that* in authority. (No warrant officers were
appointed.) So we went, a sinister adult Stalky and Co., to the
young officer who had been put in command of our Section and
told him that we could not work with any enthusiasm under the
sergeant appointed. Our meeting took place clandestinely, in a
shrubbery outside the Officers' Mess. The officer—he was little
more than a boy, I remember—was nearly as awed by the
occasion as we were. It was his first miniature command and
he looked as though he would have preferred a platoon of
tough rebellious recruits from Liverpool.

"But you can't choose your own sergeant!" he said plain-
tively.

We weren't trying to, we protested, though it was of course

exactly what we were trying to do. Perhaps the young officer had formed his own conclusions about the sergeant for he said, "I'll think it over. Better not say anything about this. I ought to put you all on a charge, I suppose."

A few mornings later the offensive sergeant was moved to another section and we were given a pleasant intelligent plump young man called Eve, who became one of us.

[6]

The Section, thus reconstituted to our taste, was sent to Glasgow to be attached to the port Section there 'for experience.' We found that, as usual in FS, the Section there had nested down comfortably and we shared their quarters and duties for two or three weeks. The most congenial of these duties was that of boarding ships from a launch, armed with a bound copy of a Black List, to check immigrants or crew. It was an unnecessary duplication of work, for the Immigration Authorities did the job with far more information and experience to go on, but it was fun racing about the harbour in a launch and climbing the Jacob's ladder of foreign ships to be offered, usually, the ship's hospitality.

When the Ferry from Ireland came in I remember once finding a Japanese among the passengers, entered in the books as an expert on poultry-farming. Surely, I said to the NCO who was tutoring me, here was a case for investigation?

"Is he in the Black Book?"

I was bound to admit that the name Hiroshima, or whatever it was, did not actually figure there.

"That's it, then," said the more experience NCO. "We're not actually at war with Japan."

We were not, for another few months. I suppose this literal-minded interpretation was inevitable, but it seemed very disappointing when so obvious—as I thought then—an enemy agent was passing through the check point into England without even an examination of his papers. I learnt more about the Rules after that.

There was an afternoon of windy springtime weather when four of us, Eve the youthful sergeant, Morley-Mower, Julyan Pickering, and I, having no duties, decided to go out of the town to the hilly countryside, to the north-west I think it was, but it may have been south-east for all I know of the country round Glasgow. We went by bus—or could it have been tram? —to a point beyond the last houses. From there the day becomes vivid in memory, for we tramped into the hills, in our Army boots and greatcoats, *for pleasure.*

There was only a streak or two of pale sunlight and the clouds had a windswept oysterish look about them, but to us, escaping from the grimy city, escaping for a while from the Army itself, it was a paragon of days and the grey hills were bright with colour and the wheeling curlews with their melancholy cry were songbirds. We were no longer soldiers wearing significant stripes, we were Belloc's Four Men coming into our own, free, expansive, boastful maybe, but not of anything connected with our lives in the Army.

We talked into the wind of books, the kind of talk in which we named our favourite authors and the books we liked to re-read, and each said to the rest of us that we *must* read this or that, though our recommendations were not smart or fashionable at the time. We shouted Army songs and complained that they had become refined in the present war as they had grown more popular outside the Army, and that the chorus of *A Troopship was Leaving Bombay* had become 'bless 'em all' so that it could be sung in any company, a betrayal of the ill-used India serviceman who had made the song. Morley-Mower repeated the words of a gorgeous lyric called *They're Digging up Father's Grave to Make a Sewer.*

The four of us felt a huge contentment and sense of comradeship overwhelming us as we walked. It was one of those momentary, haphazard companionships of Army life, evanescent and unrepeatable, but at the time powerful against all comers and eventualities. We all went different ways shortly after that afternoon and partly through coincidence I have met two of those men briefly since the war, but not the third, for Morley-Mower was killed in North Africa. We had little in common except that we all loved books, but for an hour or two we had everything in common and loved one another as brothers.

Then just as the evening began to darken a miracle happened, or what I see now as a miracle. There were few cars on the lonely road we had chosen but one came up from behind us and stopped. A young roebuck, not long dead, was roped to the open boot, and the driver, a man of some thirty-five or forty years with his small son, invited us to have a lift. It was not a large car but its owner assured us that 'we hadn't far to go'. To where? we wondered. We clambered in somehow, accepting this godsend as a welcome but quite logical eventuality in a perfect day.

Our benefactor drove us to his house of which I can remember only that it was roomy and overlooked the Clyde estuary and then, without asking who we were or what we were doing on a lonely road at nightfall or whether we were under orders to be somewhere else, he produced a bottle of whisky, poured three fingers for each of us and put out a supply of cigarettes. He never did ask those questions, or any others; he made nothing of his hospitality or of our gratitude. He was not interested in our identities, military or civilian, and seemed content to behave as though we were men he had met at his club and asked home to take pot luck. His wife, when she appeared, was no less spontaneously hospitable and produced a large meal for all of us in an hour or so. We ate as we were expected to eat, ravenously, and drank more whisky and sang choruses round the piano.

I would say that the whole of that afternoon had been imagined or romanticized by me if I had not found that long after the war the others remembered it in all its splendour.

[7]

Soon after that we were moved on to Gourock where we were billeted in a private house and had a motherly Scots landlady just like civilians who might be staying there. But we were instructed to go to a transit station in Greenock for meals and here we were to eat out of mess-tins in a gloomy Mess, formerly a meeting-hall of some kind, which stank of stale food and unwashed humanity. I suppose it was the first time I had been subjected to the more degrading conditions of Army catering and I rebelled in the only way I could—by walking out.

*　　*　　*

The ordinary soldier of the First World War had to undergo such appalling conditions, not only in the trenches but even in training, that anything we had to face would seem pampered luxury to him. But there were still times and places when our predicament was intolerable. I blame no one but Hitler and realize that in a vast citizen army built up at such comparatively short notice, ordinary standards of human comfort, cleanliness, feeding and physical well-being could not always be maintained and that much was attempted and much achieved to promote them. But I was at the time, and still am, impatient with the attitude of those who suggest that there is some virtue in privation, with the person who says 'that's what you should have *expected* from the Army', as though that excused it all. I did expect it but I was not reconciled to it, and in my own way unobtrusively did everything I could to avoid disgusting conditions in eating, and such abominations as communal defecation, or the squalor that came from inadequate water supply. Other hardships, intense cold or heat, rough sleeping conditions, boredom or fatigue I could stand, but not these.

Admittedly, as a Field Security NCO with a trickle of occasional funds from my 'civilian occupation' I was in a good position to avoid them. At Greenock, for example, I found a decent little café a few doors away and received only the reproof of a fellow lance-corporal curiously named Uff, who told me and Julyan, who walked out with me, that we were 'snobs'. It took a deal of contrivance and occasional hunger to be able to say, as I can say, that in my three years of uncommissioned service I never ate out of a mess-tin, having a particular and no doubt idiosyncratic distaste for its metal which, however much scrubbed and polished and freed from the grease left by previous owners, made the food repugnant to me.

This attitude gave a certain liveliness to the struggle to secure decent conditions in all the various surroundings in which I found myself in that year, a pull-devil pull-baker struggle between invisible authority and a thoroughly sentient and sometimes hungry individual in uniform. My friends were more tolerant of circumstances and left the tactics to me though they were appreciative of my success. There were triumphs, when outside agencies like the driver of that car on our memorable walk intervened to give us an hour or two of luxury, and there were defeats like the transit station at Greenock. But we had as allies almost the whole civilian population of Scotland, I sometimes thought. The inescapable hospitality of housewives who appeared with cups of tea and cakes at unexpected moments, of bus-conductors who risked their jobs by refusing to accept fares, of many other performers of acts of ingenious kindness, was almost embarrassing. And from a distance of thirty years I salute, if any of them are still alive and chance to read this, those—mostly elderly—ladies who waited on chilly railway-station platforms to supply hot coffee free to us on those interminable blacked-out train journeys to and from the North. And to . . . but the list is long. Soldiers in uniform in 1941 still had a faint glamour inherited from their fathers who had made real sacrifices in 1914–18 and still roused the noble attribute of Charity in those who were probably suffering hardships no lighter than theirs.

I found, in my private campaign for better conditions for me and my friends, that I needed a cool head, a good deal of impudence, a ready tongue to cover irregularities of behaviour or explain my whereabouts or absence, a delight in the rewards of these for their own sake, a positive appreciation for warmth, food, drink and entertainment and a faculty for taking risks to obtain them. Whatever else I learnt in my period of training I certainly acquired all these and they stood me in good stead throughout my Army life, even after I became an officer. I had first learned the elements in the depot at Winchester and on my various excursions from there perfected them. I am not proud of this but not in any way ashamed, for it seemed a logical way of getting the best from life and harmed no one.

It was particularly useful at Gourock where we had virtually nothing to do. I suppose it has become a mighty city now and that the town I remember of ugly red villas has disappeared among the vast blocks of flats. It was not beautiful but it was cheerful that Spring and I found a congenial bar overlooking the docks where naval officers congregated and talked with far greater discretion than officers in the Army. Better training in security, perhaps.

[8]

After Gourock, as at the end of all excursions in that year, back to the Winchester depot, but now it was as an Old Boy revisiting his school. I remembered those far-off days, nearly three months before, when I had worn an RP arm-band, and now gave a patronizing nod of acknowledgment as I passed the police post half an hour after time and did not bother to see that my name was entered at five minutes before it. "How do you get on with *Hush*?" I asked the new editor, privately considering that the numbers he had produced were not up to those 'in my time'. I slept late whenever CSM Drakely or some other Terror was calling the roll on early parade, secure in the confidence that for old friendship's sake he would tick my name.

I caused a dramatic and I believe lasting rift between the barmaid of the Southgate, a rather lovely tall blonde, and a lieutenant of some other unit who was 'taking her out'. Perhaps to show his importance or perhaps out of natural officiousness, he called me up from the dart-board and told me to hook up the collar of my battle-dress while I was playing, to remember I was in uniform and not to behave sloppily in a public place—a string of clichés habitually used to impress. I went on playing but behind me I could hear the loud and angry voice of the barmaid giving her friend hell for 'showing-off', a nice example of what is paradoxically called feminine logic as applied to military affairs.

"What did you want to interfere for? He wasn't doing you any harm."

The reply was inaudible.

"Not in here, you won't. Not while I'm here. He's a customer, same as anyone else. It wasn't as though he was misbehaving."

There were more inaudible protestations from the officer.

"Anyone would think you'd got nothing better to do than throw your weight about. Can't he have a game of darts without you interfering? You don't *own* the bar, you know."

This was all music to me. I had my share of anti-officer bias.

"If anyone's going to tell anyone how to behave, *I* am. I don't care what your duty is. It's all the same to me whether you're an officer or not. No, I *won't* come out with you this evening. Best thing you can do is go home and next time you come in here mind your own business."

An event this, by the standards of eventfulness in Army life.

CHAPTER FOUR

The Smoke

[1]

I WAS given leave four times before being drafted abroad for the remainder of the war in 1942. I spent most of the time in London and I must be among a good many thousand service men for whom London in the first three years of war was not only—perhaps not even so much—the blitzed city as the home town which welcomed them on leave. Of the blitz itself I saw little more than the results. In this I was lucky, hearing the sirens only three or four times while I was there. But the changes the blitz had brought about in people, in habits, in surroundings, in the whole way of life in the capital were sharply evident.

To come on leave was to find a new London which had sprung up in less than three years since I had lived there. To outward view as well as in spirit it had changed. The crowd that moved along its pavements was cosmopolitan—foreign and Commonwealth uniforms seeming to outnumber our own, for the Londoners on leave wore civvies when they could. The bush-hats of lean sharp-eyed Australians, the smart uniforms of self-assured Canadians, the neat grey of the Polish troops predominated. The French looked grim, even their sailors with coquettish red pom-poms on their caps might have been wondering that this strangely festive city could exist at all while France lay prone across the Channel, though in liquor they became as frivolously cheerful as the rest.

As a soldier I thought that civilians showed an extraordinary spirit of good nature and friendliness, extraordinary in view of what they had suffered and were suffering from the blitz.

61

Strangers talked to one another with no provocation, old women were sometimes embarrassed by acts of spontaneous kindness, and anyone with a tale to tell, even of calamity, got a hearing in public places, on buses and in the Underground. I found ostentatious cordiality was everywhere, concealing, I supposed, the tiredness and despondency which people were determined not to show. Friends of mine of settled disposition were almost unrecognizable, for even if they were not in uniform they had formed new habits and talked another language. Even my service friends on leave were different from the dutiful soldiers I had known, reverting to a civilian self-importance or to their pre-war character as a heavy father or carefree law-breaker, unconscious now of distinctions of rank, hobnobbing with a Major General father-in-law perhaps, or displaying an attractive wife.

In the daytime I saw with relief old landmarks, half-surprised that Harrods or the pub on the corner, the statue of Shakespeare in Leicester Square Garden or a favourite all-night coffee-stall was still there, and I marvelled at the shops which continued to offer peacetime goods and treat their customers with peacetime respectfulness. Indeed anything that continued more or less unchanged was surprising in this extraneous new city and I would greet with astonished delight a publican who had kept his place behind a remembered bar or the doorman I had known of a hotel or cinema.

The war had changed the press and the radio news-bulletin but even more the public attitude to them. News had been a daily entertainment for most people—now it was a regular draught that had to be swallowed, half medicine half elixir, and a friend would leave me 'to be home in time to hear the six o'clock news'. There was no topical song at that time, however, *Washing on the Siegfried Line* having turned out to be a damp squib and *Lily Marlene* not having arrived yet.

It was at night when this unfamiliar London became most hectically strange and for me exciting. The silence of many of the streets was macabre and even in what was still called the

West End, the sound of the scarce and faltering traffic did not drown the beat of heavy boots on the pavement or the noise of the multilingual crowd. People moved uncertainly, looking for the name of a street they were already in, or for one another. Eyes met in the half-darkness and a sympathy was formed sufficient for the rest of the night. Faces came out of the black-out and passed, each one a lost opportunity; attachments were formed in a barside conversation of minutes which might last for the rest of the war, or longer. Everyone wanted to meet someone else, it seemed, whether known or unknown, man or woman, and we were all intent on promiscuity. Whores were plentiful but they found it hard to face the competition of a self-sufficiently profligate society seeking immediate pleasure within its own resources.

There was drunkenness, but arising from too much good fellowship; not the weak and guilty sottishness of alcoholics, for it was boisterous, disorderly, sometimes dangerous and always excused. That there were crimes of violence in the black-out and mean thefts I knew, but the general desire was for pleasure, brief gratifications, laughter, companionship and new experience.

As soon as I experienced it I decided that I would not try to recapture the happiness I had known in my former life here, or look for old friends or re-create the past among them, but I would go out full of released energy and appetite to enjoy surroundings insistently inviting and hitherto unknown.

[2]

On my first leave, after seeing that my dog was happy and well in Pershore, I went down to Hertfordshire to visit my mother. I found her, now that she was entering her eighties, still doing her daily crossword, still playing Chopin and Beethoven on the piano, and still talking to her acquaintances of her five children, this time boasting that they were all in uniform. I noticed that in her conventionally romanticizing mind even her eldest son, my brother Ronald who had died in 1937, had become 'really a casualty of the 1914–18 war—he was so badly gassed'. I tried to convince her that children in uniform were nothing to be proud of—rather the contrary. She might have boasted if one of us had gone to America to write poetry or become a civil servant, but our form of escapism was not considered at all *chic*. It was no good. She only wanted to tell me again that my older brother was in the RAF in Iceland, my sister an officer in the WRAF, and that my two younger brothers, having returned from France at the time of Dunkirk, now had commissions. The implication, which she was at pains not to voice, was that I was rather shamefully behind in the family race for promotion shown in framed photographs on my mother's mantelpiece, but a lot could be excused to me on account of the unmartial nature of my pre-war life.

"Wouldn't they give you a commission as an Interpreter?" she asked rather wistfully. A lance-corporal was such a very unglamorous visitor to Little Gaddesden. But she cheered up when I told her the nature of Field Security and thereafter spoke of my job as 'very hush-hush'.

[3]

I owe much of the deep and memorable pleasure of those leaves in London to one man who gave me the hospitality of his home. He would have seemed before the war a most unlikely host for he was not a relative or even a friend of long standing and he was under no obligation to befriend and give shelter to me.

His name was Peter Noble and he had worked for me for a short time as a secretary while I was travelling with the circus,

but he was an ambitious many-sided young man, fascinated by
the entertainment world, and now that this world was throwing
up easy or premature reputations on all sides from among the
artists, actors, critics and literary hangers-on who remained in
London, he was making a niche for himself as an energetic
enthusiast for all the arts and an associate of their masters. He
was a born hero-worshipper and missionary, preaching the pre-
eminence of those he admired and not, it must be admitted,
forgetting himself, though his good-natured and sunny
disposition saved him from appearing an egotistic climber.

He had gone through an adolescent dallying with com-
munism and on the outbreak of war had firmly declared himself a conscientious objector, an act of sincerity which doubtless
needed as much courage in that time of excitement and un-
certainty as a thoughtless rush to the nearest recruiting station.
He was now in the AFS and had a flat in North London where
he spent what time he could spare from his work as fireman
and his dedicated service to entertainment, his membership of
a score of small societies and clubs, his occasional contributions
to ephemeral weeklies, his interviewing of stars, his busy life on
the outskirts of the world he loved. After the war he came into
his own as a showbiz journalist, a married man and a father, but
I have only seen him once briefly since that year for this was a
wartime relationship of generous hospitality on his side and
gratitude on mine.

I did not more than sporadically share his interests, for I had
put behind me what career I had for the duration and scarcely
wrote a word from the time of joining the army till my release,
though in nostalgic moods I enjoyed hearing the current news
and gossip and Peter insisted that there was a 'lot going on'.
This seemed to be true—ballet was booming as I would see for
myself, and literature, Peter said, had all sorts of new outlets,
revolutionary editors and a public greedy for new names. He
took me to see Unity Theatre's pantomime and wanted to
introduce me to several of John Lehmann's authors, or contributors to even more esoteric periodicals, and urged me to

E

write something which would keep my small reputation in existence. But I was delighting in my philistinism and wanted, as I told him, to 'relax and enjoy my leave' which I should not do if I was expected to react intelligently. He accepted that and let me go to see an occasional revue or an undemanding and unfashionable film, or more often to cruise about the streets and find what entertainment I could. He was an ideal host, never questioning my hours or objecting to an unforeseen companion in my room.

[4]

Among Peter's friends, young men and girls active in the arts, keener on understanding the politics of the war than following its progress, determined not to succumb to the pressure to enlist in one of the services, talkative, cheerful and eager to act, write, paint or make music while the going was good, I found one enchanting quality, their sympathy with me who they thought had been forced to abandon all this, their kindness and generosity to all servicemen whom they imagined to be the victims of inhuman deprivation. They saw no merit in military service but they were conscious of having so much that I had not, their privacy, their own homes, a degree of freedom to follow their own pursuits, comfortable beds and chairs and warm firesides. Perhaps they exaggerated the vexations of Army life; they certainly wanted to do all they could for me, sew on a button or buy a drink according to their sex, or in more directly physical ways make my leave eventful. For in this way, unlike that of 1914–18, the distinction was not between soldiers and 'slackers', or between those offering themselves for sacrifice and conscientious objectors; now we were all conscientious objectors, and all in it. The distinction was between those who could continue to live at home and press on with their private ambitions and those who could not.

Peter Noble and his friends were poor, but they found means to give me a good time. All my pre-war friends had scattered; my flat, abandoned on the outbreak of war, had now been destroyed by bombs, and I had no family home. The young people I met through Peter were previously unknown to me, but they adopted me as though I was a stray, and the adventure of exploring blacked-out London did the rest.

Leave from one of the services was an occasion for a bachelor to regret not having married, if not for sentimental reasons, then certainly for practical ones. I was not much stirred by the old army spiel of 'what I shall do to the wife when I get home', with all its lubricious details, but for the first time I saw drawbacks in my unattached condition. Most of the men and women of my own age or younger to whom I had given what I had to give of affection and loyalty were in the Services or out of London, and when I tried their telephone numbers strangers answered, or there was no answer at all. I had no close friends in my own profession except Louis Golding who had gone to America to work on a film which was never made. John Hitchcock was in Birmingham, already a key man in the nickel and consequently the arms business. Molly Fordham was abroad somewhere as a correspondent for the *News Chronicle*— she was killed in the next year. Myles Eadon, who had shared my flat, and Barton Wills were both commissioned, serving 'somewhere in England' and Arnold Taylor, the only one of my cousins I knew well, had sold his farm and joined the Navy—he went down on the *Hood* that summer. The Rosaires, depleted by Ivor having joined the Army and become a PT instructor, were tenting somewhere under great difficulties and Ted Scamp the gypsy who had travelled with me had temporarily and understandably disappeared. Michael Harrison was in North Africa, Richard Blake Brown was a naval chaplain and his brother Lincoln was working down in Oxfordshire.

Not only the inhabitants but the focal points of my pre-war curriculum had vanished or changed out of recognition. The

Chinese restaurant in which I ate so often and so well had disappeared, leaving its sign over an empty basement, and when I went, expecting some at least of the familiar faces, to the domino room of the Café Royal there was no one I had ever seen before. Only Roy Hardy, of all my pre-war friends, remained in London and he could never have been persuaded to leave it. I used to think he *was* London.

So if it had not been for Peter Noble and his circle I should have been pretty lonely on leave and perhaps would have had nowhere to stay in London but the Union Jack Club. But when I remember Peter's friends coming into the weird half-light of Waterloo Station to see me off on my way back to the Winchester depot I feel that I was as well cared-for as anyone.

[5]

I suppose the Army arrested my development or stressed the evergreen immaturity of my outlook. I was ten years older than most of the men I trained with and the friends I made on leave, and I had travelled, written, lived with more vicissitudes than most of them, yet I was if anything more callow in heart and mind. This was a blessed defect for when later I was attached to infantry units and lived with tougher and more ordinary soldiers, I could lose myself wholly in the fitful chances, the earnest conversations, the petty triumphs of Army life and appreciate the characters of semi-illiterate comrades in their early twenties. Even at this time, on leave in London, I could sympathize with the enthusiasms and troubles of younger people, not as a more experienced man but as one of themselves. Childish is the word that may be applied, with unkind intent, to the emotions and exhilarations I felt with younger people and in an unliteral sense I accept it. My enjoyment of new pleasures, new sights and sounds and people had the wholeheartedness of a child's pleasure and I remember them without any restraint, without any shamefaced admission that these were not for a man of thirty-seven years who had earned his own living for two decades. I was happy among my juniors and remained so throughout the war and longer, not with any *faux jeune* self-consciousness or fixed intent, but because it was my natural ambience.

For instance there was a group of young dancers who were appearing with the Ballet Rambert in a strange wartime entertainment called Lunch-time Ballet at the Ambassadors Theatre. Is it remembered still, I wonder? It gave enormous pleasure to Londoners who could not go to the theatre at night and even inspired a revue song, *I Like a Little Ballet with my Lunch*. I do not know how many of its items have reappeared since those afternoon occasions, Ninette de Valois's *Bar aux Folies Bergère*, André Howard's *Capriol Suite* with Peter Warlock's music almost certainly, and perhaps Frederick Ashton's *Foyer de Danse* for which Gerald Berners wrote the music, and Frank Staff's *Peter and the Wolf*.

Leo Kersley, whom I had met before the war through having bought a portrait of him by Clifford Hall, was dancing in several of these (he was the Wolf in the last-named, a brilliant bit of grotesquerie), and I used to go with him and Celia Franca and Peter Franklin-White and other girls and boys from the company to the incredible *confiserie* of Madame Floris, who fed us on cream cakes and chocolate eclairs, luxuries which had almost disappeared in that year. Tempestuous chatter over cakes, mad, lovely movements from the girls, though I daresay the conversation was infantile. Lunch-time Ballet and all that went with it filled many of my afternoons before the nightly black-out came down and the long evening began.

There were other entertainments at unusual times; a midnight theatre, as I remember it underground, but it may have been in a semi-basement, where a small audience of twenty or thirty stood along the bar at the back of the hall or secured one of the few seats to watch a series of turns on the miniature

stage and a masterful woman who ran the place introduced
each of them. Peter Ustinov, then a gauche and very foreign
young man, made what I believe was his first professional appearance, doing some energetic impersonations.

These two shows had come into being because of abnormal
conditions. More in the tradition of the London theatre but
certainly no less unforgettable was Harry Kendall's revue *Rise
Above It* at the Comedy, for which, I see now from an old
programme, my friends Val Guest and David Fairweather
wrote some of the lyrics, and the two Hermiones (Gingold and
Baddeley) most gloriously disported themselves and Georgina
Cookson and Walter Grisham appeared.

But the theatre, though it has given me all I could ask of rich
entertainment and splendid memories, has never been a com-
pulsive passion with me, and more often than not while I was
on leave I was satisfied to go to pubs. Their atmosphere in that
year was unforgettable and to this day in certain London bars a
middle-aged man will look round him and say—'I used to come
here during the war, you know', with reminiscent affection.
One came into their brilliance from the black streets and felt no
surprise at anything one might see—three French sailors defiantly
enjoying a drunken song, a lachrymose woman describing not
some tragedy of war but the breakage of a bottle in the black-
out, a pianist in drag, a CMP patrol looking for victims, James
Agate with a couple of guardsmen less conspicuous now that
they wore battle-dress, a well-known broadcaster cheerfully
intoxicated, using the language he had had to suppress before
the microphone, sulky whores complaining of their misfortunes, a group of servicemen of several nationalities hugging
one another with inebriate passion, unable to speak one another's languages, violent quarrels and occasional fights,
hysteria, obscenity, gentleness, sudden love, sudden outraged
departures. I thought once incongruously how my friend
Ernst Thoma of Cologne would have enjoyed this, how all
Germans would have loved this beery brotherliness and how
lonely they must sometimes feel without an ally whom they

could respect, without another nation to sing with, and only their dreary little undersexed rabble-rouser to romanticize.

I had learned from an experienced old soldier met in a pub in the Tottenham Court Road to send a telegram to the depot with a prepaid reply asking for an extension of leave, supporting it with some cryptic *cri de cœur* like 'Brother on leave 18th inst apply extension leave to 20/6/41'. Or 'Important interview publishers 19th inst apply extension leave to 20/6/41'. It never failed to secure three or four extra days; more than that was not wise to demand. But it ended at last at Waterloo Station, and leaving London was like going back to school twenty years earlier.

It was consoling to know after those first four months of delay at Winchester that there too I had friends and I quote a scribbled note that was awaiting me on one occasion when I reached the depot, because it voices exactly the preoccupations of those days.

Wednesday

Dear Rupert,
      Your kit is on the top berth of a bed in room no 32 where I have fixed for you to sleep tonight. I am in room 33. Tomorrow morning 267 Section parades 8.45 for a day's motor cycling. Incidentally your name is likely to be called at roll call as Aitken is orderly sergeant and he has a list of people returning. Anyhow I don't suppose that will worry you.

Julyan

CHAPTER FIVE

Combined Operations

[1]

It must have been in May when my friend Morley-Mower told me that we were both to report that afternoon to a certain officer whose name, Annis, was unknown to us. Morley had discovered the reason for this and confided it with some excitement.

"He's the OC 29 Section. It's for Combined Operations." This was an unfamiliar term as yet but Morley was like someone inspired by it. He had a romantic view of the war.

"Combined Ops!" he repeated ardently. "It's a thing to be in."

Annis was a goodlooking young fellow with a dark spruce moustache to match his dark eyes. He was not long commissioned and drafted to Field Security because of the languages he claimed. He could be seen at once, by the sort of perception developed in the Army, as being easy-going, unofficious, reasonably amicable, in other words *not* a shit. Some of these qualities might be—indeed later turned out to be—two-edged, for if he was too obliging with senior officers his section would suffer, but so far as I knew then he was all right.

"I understand," he said, "that you have been recommended for a commission."

This was the first I had heard of it—it was certainly not by Matlock. I let it pass, wondering what would come of this unusual conversation.

"There's a vacancy for a sergeant in my section. If you join it I can have you made up."

Join it? What talk was this? I had not been given an option in anything since I enlisted. But I hesitated. A sergeant's rank was lofty, seen from my own, but it was a dead end if one thought in terms of promotion. Moreover it would entail some responsibility and could bring about separation, however unwilling, from the friends with whom I had grumbled rebelliously for months. But it meant slightly better pay and that had become a serious consideration now that pre-war funds were exhausted, and it would bring certain trivial privileges with the alleviation of a few minor discomforts. On the whole then, yes. A sergeant in a Section attached to Combined Operations, an immediate departure from Winchester, activity and travel (prosaically called movement), worse fates could be meted out at the depot.

I had never been a prefect at school and did not realize the sense of betrayal I should be made to feel by those who had trained with me. When I moved up to the Sergeants' Mess, in which those mighty men the instructors ate and relaxed, Eddie Bates their orderly would no longer speak to me. Another man had expected my job and complained most bitterly to all listeners that I had jumped the queue through having 'got in with' the powers in the depot, that I had no experience (as he had) of Section work and very little of anything else to do with the Army. Morley-Mower had not been chosen to join the Section because of language deficiencies and although he did not take it out on me and laughed at my three stripes, he was a disappointed man. Even Julyan looked at me with no sympathy at all.

That promotion opened a long, personal and sometimes bitter antagonism, with a few pitched battles and a lot of guerrilla warfare, between me and the Sergeant-Major of the Section, a man named Heacock. The very formation of an FS Section was partly responsible for this, since for each there was an officer who might or might not know anything about Intelligence, and a sergeant-major who was not expected to, but was responsible for the discipline, pay, quarters and transport of the two sergeants and ten lance-corporals, trained in security, under him.

Heacock had been a regular in a Lancashire Regiment and had earned his CSM's rank with years of slogging and efficiency, an unusually good man in the office or on the square and a proficient soldier. He believed in Army methods and regarded the whole business of security work as something ornamental and extraneous, too often used to usurp privileges and secure ease and comfort by those who had not earned the right to them —as of course they often were. He was not an unlikeable or a dishonest man, but he could see only one way, the Army way, in which anything should be done and he was obstinately determined to follow it.

In this he lacked the firm support of an officer, an essential for the maintenance of discipline as he had always known it. Annis was, as I had guessed, too easy-going to defend Heacock in his literal interpretation of petty orders and asked only for a smooth-running Section in which Security work could be done without too much regimentation. So that the struggle between Heacock and me was not only one between two human beings but between the traditional Army code and a badly disciplined interloper, between what Heacock knew to be Correct and what one scatty so-called sergeant wanted. For nearly two years while we both remained with the Section the advantage went sometimes to him, sometimes to me, but we both saw the necessity of respecting appearances and nobody, not even Annis, realized more than vaguely what was going on.

Years later, when I was a Field Security Officer in India, Heacock came to see me, and I am glad to say we were able to laugh over the lethal warfare in which we had engaged and he went so far as to admit that he had paid too much attention to bumph, and I that I had behaved, by Army standards, disgracefully. But there was no laughing over it at the time.

We had thought to leave the depot immediately, but as usual we waited. No Army song was ever more apt than *Why Are We Waiting?* sung mournfully to the tune of *Adeste Fideles*. Weeks passed during which we had nothing to do but speculate on the future. FS men were given no prior information unknown to others but they had a useful clue to their destination abroad in the foreign language common to all members of the Section, in our case Spanish. What Spanish-speaking territory was about to be the scene of a Combined Operation, we asked ourselves, and our guess ranged from South America to Rio de Oro, from the Spanish mainland to the Canary Isles. All of them seemed alluring in the dank spring weather and the constrictive regime of the depot.

At last on a day of teeming rain we set out on our newly issued Matchless motor cycles, armed with totally unmanageable .45 revolvers, our kitbags in the back of the officer's miniature truck. Heacock had learned one Security lesson—he did not even tell his Section to what part of England we were heading or let us know that we should stop in Worcester for lunch, for which we had been issued with ration money. It appeared that neither he nor Annis was a skilled map-reader for at one o'clock, believing that we had reached Worcester, he pulled up in the middle of the square at Pershore, right opposite the Angel, the farmers' pub which I had left little more than six months before. I remember that there was no time to disencumber ourselves of our soaking mackintosh coverings and we left puddles in the dining-room in which last summer I had lunched several times a week. But last summer belonged to a previous incarnation.

That afternoon we reached Chester and a rendezvous of some kind failed so that we stood about for three hours in a station yard and *waited*. Annis had gone to report at some headquarters or other and Heacock *had no orders*. This was a ghastly situation for any regular soldier and he looked baffled and miserable, not because he had a dozen hungry men with their motor bikes and packs to dispose of—they should expect this sort of thing—but because *having no orders*, he did not know what to do. The afternoon was somewhat cheered for me when I recognized Rollo Baker whom I had taught in a preparatory school twenty years before, now a major in the RA. We chatted for a few moments, but he *did* know what to do and drove away followed by formidable-looking gun-carriages. For another hour or two, until night fell, we waited, then Heacock at last consulted the Town Major or Movement Control officer, and we found ourselves in filthy civilian lodgings, still unfed.

I did not mind sleeping on the ground, on sacking, on a hard bunk, in a railway goods van or in the back of a lorry, all of which I achieved in the Army, but dirty bed-clothes and a rancid atmosphere I could not stand and slept that night fully dressed on the unopened bed I was told to occupy. Next day, through a friendly member of the town FS Section, I found myself a billet, and though Heacock considered that this practically amounted to mutiny and would lead to endless trouble with the billeting officer when discovered, I managed to retain it while we were in Chester. It was in a pub of cherished memory called the Green Dragon.

[2]

We had come to Chester to *wait* and we did so for some weeks. The sunny shores of Rio de Oro, or wherever we imagined we were bound for, receded, but we had only the Sergeant-Major and his preoccupation with work-tickets and log-books (by which our petrol supply was limited), to restrict our scope.

I do not seem to have taken those restrictions very seriously for a I made a number of excursions from Chester, whether with official sanction or not I cannot remember, to see people and places out of the range of permitted motor cycling.

First I went to Liverpool by the Mersey Tunnel, which had been built since I had my first teaching job in New Brighton at the age of seventeen. The effect of the blitz could be nowhere more appalling than in Liverpool, I thought, looking for landmarks and finding truncated buildings and rubble where they had stood. Except for London, this city, full of crudely nostalgic associations for me, was the only place I knew well enough to grieve over and in that early summer of 1941 it looked desolated beyond imagining.

I had come to find Julyan Pickering who was here *waiting* with a Section bound for North Africa. I discovered him with others I had known at Winchester in an empty house left standing alone among the ruins, and we escaped to a pub to celebrate this brief reunion. Later he came to Chester for a week-end, such visiting between members of FS Sections not being too difficult. He eventually went overseas in the following year.

On another expedition from Chester, this time on two days' unofficial leave, I went to Llandudno to see that magnificent old man John Bayley, a miner's son who became a teacher and in the 1880s started his own school at Wellington, Shropshire. I spent my sixteenth and seventeenth years as a pupil there before John Bayley sold it for a hundred thousand pounds and it became Wrekin College. Now, a knighted nonagenarian (he died in 1952, five months short of his hundredth birthday), he was living at Llandudno and preparing an extraordinary pamphlet which he later sent out 'To my Loyal Friends, the dear Old Boys of Wellington College (now Wrekin College), Shropshire'. It read like one of his speeches, full of subjunctive clauses which never rejoined the sentence, rhetorical, biblical and to a reader who could not hear in imagination the vigorous old writer enunciating them, absurd.

He was upstairs when I arrived and I heard him singing as he came down. He had been playing golf, he said, and making the only admission of his own senescence I ever heard from him, added—"I can't manage more than nine holes nowadays."

After that visit I decided on a bolder, more illicit one to Pershore where the gypsies would be gathered for the pea-picking as in the previous year. I had no scruples about using WD petrol for this bit of joy-riding; I would have been superhumanly conscientious if I had, for in the Army the only individuals who could afford to indulge in ethics were the very high ranking. But I realized the risk of detection for I was going a hundred miles or more out of the district to which I was limited without official excuse or alibi if I was stopped by the CMP or any other inquisitive body.

All went well, however, and I found the Locks encamped in the same corner of the same orchard as they occupied every year and their eldest son on leave, his rifle incongruously propped against the tent pole.

On my way back to Chester I gave some suggestion of legality to the excursion by having dinner at the Ludlow Arms with an Intelligence officer, Sir Philip Magnus the biographer. This was of vital assistance to me when I came to explain my absence to Heacock, for whom the authority of an officer, writer or no, was always sufficient.

There was another of those play-acting Security Exercises in which I had to take the part of an enemy agent, this time against the Home Guard in the Wirral Peninsula. I went by motor cycle to Wallasey and succeeded in entering their headquarters, a private house, without much difficulty, since lying for the purpose of these exercises had become as easy to me as lying to cover up my own transgressions. I gathered the usual stock of information but had to remain in the district until midnight when the exercise was over. I was about to return to Chester when I was questioned by two Home Guardsmen who asked me to come back to headquarters. This I did to see the face of the CO when I returned. But he refused to acknowledge that the time set for the exercise was long finished and insisted on regarding me as captured. It was significant of the time, and of my total immersion in Army affairs, that I was as indignant about this injustice as Colonel Blimp was in a similar predicament in the film of his Life. All sense of normal proportion in human affairs being dead, I cursed the Home Guardsmen of Wallasey as cheats and bad losers. And when I slept in a YMCA at Birkenhead that night my wallet, with two weeks' pay in it, was stolen from the uniform hanging beside me. "Oh we get a lot of that sort of thing", said the overworked and honorary superintendent when I complained.

[3]

Our move from Chester when it came was sudden. That must have been the experience of nearly everyone in our blinkered Army—we waited, kicking our heels somewhere, or settled down comfortably in a place as though we would live there for the rest of our lives; then abruptly from invisible unpredictable authorities came an order to move. In the purgatory between Civilian and Army life which was our existence in Field Security this seemed more shattering than if we lived in barracks or under canvas. Washing had to be obtained from a civilian laundry, farewells made to the kindly people we had met and extraneous articles pressed into a kitbag.

But this time, the rumour ran with a good deal of confirming evidence, it was the Real Thing. We were going somewhere, doing something, at least connected with the war if it was not part of it.

If I had been in Heacock's confidence, as I very certainly was not, he might have told me that our orders were to go on board the *Batory,* the Polish ship which had joined the Allies. We had not yet grown accustomed to distinguishing between ship-borne exercises in Combined Operations and that 'real thing', but when we found detachments of the RAF on board as well as a battalion of Royal Marines and certain other entities, anomalous in a mere exercise, we decided that this was It. As indeed it was, or was intended to be, and would have been, but for unknown factors far out of our ken.

We clanked on board that beautiful ship and found to our amazement that a splendid lunch was laid for several hundred

men in one of the dining-saloons with uniformed stewards in
attendance. This proved to be due to a misunderstanding with
the Poles on the scale of rations for ORs, and after that
occasion we were given Army food which had to be dished out
by our own appointed orderlies. We unpacked our kit in
cabins (six sergeants to a single cabin sleeping on wooden
structures erected where bunks had been), and settled down.

I forgot where the *Batory* lay for the next month, somewhere
in the Firth of Clyde I imagine, but during that month the
Hood was sunk and Germany invaded Russia, events which
were held to have affected our fate, and slowly the realization
spread amongst us that we were not going anywhere at all, that
whatever had been our purpose it was cancelled, that we should
go ashore again and wait.

It was nearly a year before I discovered the truth which has
long been known to war historians. The Combined Operation
for which we were intended was planned months earlier when
units of the German Army were along the Pyrenees. In case
Hitler marched into Spain, Britain would invade the Canary
Isles. Franco convinced Hitler that he could not invade the
Peninsula without opposition and by the time our force was
ready Hitler gave up the idea of attacking Spain and finalized
his plans for invading Russia.

It was as simple as that, but for us somewhere at the lowest
end of the scale, it was anticlimax. Boarding a ship had seemed
to bring us at least a little nearer to movement and the possibility of sunlight and for a time we had begun to believe in
them. Now Combined Operations seemed a phrase, like any
other Army phrase, without promise.

[4]

For me those weeks on the *Batory* were a turning-point. For
the first time I was among the men I had expected to meet when

I joined the Army and was completely at ease with them. Of the ten NCOs of my Section as finally constituted, four were schoolmasters and all but two of the remainder much-educated men. They were quite good fellows, more bookish and disciplined than I, but they did not conform to my notion of a serviceman whom I expected to be hard-drinking, hard-swearing, rather garrulous in an unintellectual way, sentimental under a tough crust, disciplined in practice but in spirit anarchic, easily moved to emotion though unconscious of it, brave, generous, grumbling—men without women, in fact, showing some of the lovable characteristics of both sexes.

Here on the *Batory* men of all three services were at their best. They believed they were going into action and welcomed it. They had made their farewells on shore and, resigned to family disunion, were volubly cheerful with one another. The Royal Marines had the most to grumble about for they had recently undergone training for a role which was not traditionally theirs, and had been formed into battalions as though they were no more than infantry, but they appeared to be the most light-hearted of us all.

There was a bar for sergeants scarcely changed from the second-class bar of peace-time cruises, which was presided over by a Polish barman. He was a big fellow who had served in the German Army as a sergeant and spoke only a little English, but some humourist had taught him to shout "Time, shentlemen, please. Haf you no homes to go to?" at ten—or was it eleven?—o'clock and he did so with good-natured gusto. Every evening we gossiped there, argued, played ha'-penny brag, and shouted choruses beloved of the Royals, and across the years I can hear them—

> No care have I to grieve me,
> No pretty little girl to deceive me,
> I'm as happy as a king, believe me,
> As I go rolling home.
> Rolling home,
> Rolling home,

Rolling home,
Rolling home,
By the light of the silvery moon,
And happy is the lass
That will let you feel her arse
As I go rolling home.

Or *Roll me over* or *When there isn't a girl about*. The bar served
no spirits—forbidden to other ranks—and only Australian
beer, but Canadian (Caporal) cigarettes were fivepence for
twenty and the beer though unfamiliar was strong.

I acquired a nickname in that bar, the only one I have ever
been given, and a nickname in the Army is worth having. It
came by chance. During our first days on board I was playing
cards with two RA sergeants and one of another unit. A
friend of the unknown sergeant spoke to him from the bar as
'Mac' and one of the Gunners thought first, that he spoke to me,
and second, that he used the name Max. A few moments later
he brought it out and I did not correct him. It caught on,
lasted till the end of the war, and even today I get letters which
address me by it.

[5]

When it was at last known that there was to be no Operation,
for the time being at least, Admiral Sir Roger Keyes, who was
in command of Combined Ops, came on the *Batory* to hold a
conference for senior officers, and our Section was given the
job of keeping would-be eavesdroppers among the troops from
the open windows of the saloon.

But I had a far bloodier task that evening—the last on
board—when all ranks were called in by ship's wireless from
the decks, from the bars, or from their cabins, to hear a
Security lecture before they would disperse for leave the next
day. Annis wisely handed over to me because in their mood

that night the mixed crowd, RAF, Royal Marines and Army, would not have listened to an officer. Only their sympathy for one of their rank made them give me a hearing and there was a shout of 'Why aren't the bleeding officers here? They need ---- ing Security'. But that was an audience worth winning. Foyle's Literary Luncheon which I had addressed two years earlier, though critical enough, was nothing to it. I don't suppose the spiel I put across prevented anyone from telling his friends and relatives the names of the ships being used for Combined Operations or where they were to be found but it might have, and it would have been good practice for me if I had thought of entering politics after the war as a prospective member for a tough constituency.

On that same last night Heacock pulled off a master-stroke. Though the whole Force was to go on leave at once, a representative of each unit had to stay on board in charge of his unit's baggage and Heacock maintained that it should be a sergeant and detailed me for the job.

But this was another of my apparent misfortunes which turn out so well. The *Batory* went into dock in Glasgow for de-gauzing and for six delightful weeks of summer I remained on board. I got leave with a lengthy extension a week after the Section had gone ashore.

I enjoyed myself enormously. I was at first rather baffled to find myself the senior NCO left on board, with the duty of calling a parade every morning of Marines, RAF, CMP and representatives of several Army units. I had never given a command or called a roll and the young second lieutenant, the only officer left, was as shy as I was. Moreover I was expected to detail men for certain light fatigues. But all that was over in an hour and the rest of the day was mine.

The Glasgow workers de-gauzing the ship wanted cigarettes and the Polish store-keeper had enough out of bond to supply me with a box of five hundred every day which meant by contemporary standards a vast profit—enough to go ashore in Glasgow twice a week and play poker with the Polish crew on most other nights. Apart from that the allowance of food and drink was lavish and there was endless leisure. The Polish purser moved me into an officer's cabin, the weather was warm and sunny, and bombing in Glasgow had ceased.

I had time for correspondence and wrote to Lord Alfred Douglas who sent me a copy of the sonnet he had written to Winston Churchill, *Not that of old I loved you over-much* . . . which healed old wounds and was acknowledged by Churchill with a brief 'Time heals all'. (Bosie had gone to prison for a criminal libel on Churchill.) It appeared in the *Daily Mail* but there was a misprint in the second line so that the cutting he sent me from a periodical called *Kingdom Come* was, he said with characteristic attention to minutiae in the matter of his work, its first appearance 'in its fully corrected form'. Bosie remained in Hove, coming up to London to address the Royal Literary Society with a virulent attack, in the manner of his most bellicose days, on the poetry of T. S. Eliot. It was pleasant to think of him in his quiet flat, engrossed in the interests of his later days, still, though rarely, writing poetry and running out to buy the evening paper to see the racing results, but it all seemed rather remote.

News of my luxurious existence reached Heacock where he was with the Section under canvas at Inverary. He realized the mistake he had made and determined to recall me. He was not a vindictive man or an unjust one—he was a stickler for discipline who resented my faculty for avoiding its ardours. He sent one of the schoolmasters down to 'replace' me, but did so rather tentatively in the absence of Annis on leave, so that I was able to send back the replacement with fair words. A week or two later Annis himself arrived to recall me, primed I gathered by Heacock. I explained, not without all justification, that there was a great deal of Security work to be done here, what with so much WD property on board, the Polish crew and the Glaswegian workers, all of which, I said, I had well in hand. I was preparing a report. No one else could pick up the threads. This worked, and Annis returned to Inverary, not fooled but persuaded that there was no point in recalling me. I do not know how he explained it all to Heacock, whose Army experience he respected. I would not have minded going but I was determined to hold out as long as I could. Heacock had left me here when he thought the job was bloody—let him realize he had dropped a clanger.

A week later the thing was settled. An NCO arrived with written orders for me to report to Annis at Inverary and I left. But—rewarding irony—I arrived to find the Section under immediate orders to embark on another ship and I did not even unpack my kit or sleep a night ashore.

[6]

The forces selected for Combined Operations had a strange amphibious existence for the best part of a year until they were used for the first of the tasks for which they were trained, the landings in Madagascar. For the lower, uninformed ranks it was puzzling to be moved on and off the troopships allotted to us, converted passenger liners mostly, never told whether our embarkation meant just another exercise or the real thing at last.

It seemed that there was nowhere for us to go, nothing to do. While troops were pouring into North Africa and other smaller theatres of war we hung about in the Lowlands of Scotland arguing about our possible future, deciding that a force of such strength and preparedness could not be kept in reserve for long. Some idiot said in print that the lion was preparing to spring but that sort of talk had—or should have—gone out in the nineteenth century and we were just a lot of impatient troops taking what leave we could get and never knowing whether or not to say good-bye.

Men professed to be bored, of course, but this was a modest way of saying that they wanted some action, a fact that could never have been admitted, or even entered the conscious mind of servicemen in this century. (Whether those of the past talked as they do in Victorian novels and old songs I cannot say, but it seems extremely doubtful.) There were periods of boredom, no doubt, and of exasperation, but generally we liked being at sea for exercises and conditions on land were better than most of us had learned to expect. We became acquainted with a wide variety of our opposite numbers in the various units, like peacetime passengers thrown together for a cruise, and had time to decide which were 'smashing fellows', which were merely 'all right', and which were shits. From our time on land we came to know the Lowlands pretty well from Inverary to Jedburgh and Hawick.

When I rejoined the Section at Inverary after my summer on the *Batory* in Glasgow docks, it was to go on board the *Winchester Castle* a ship closely associated with Combined Operations. I was on her three times for exercises and became quite fond of her. On that first occasion we did not leave Loch Fyne, I think, but as always (in the early years of the war) tobacco and beer were cheap on shipboard while for our Section the only duty was the daily inspection. In the eyes of the Section, Heacock had one special merit as a sergeant-major, he liked to 'get his head down' in the manner of most experienced soldiers and did not bother us. On most evenings I played cards, for the only time in my life, since I normally detest the sight of the things with their fish-faced kings and queens staring inanimately. In civilian life I had always thought they took up time meant for pleasanter pursuits, but on board troopships, where there was little intellectual card-playing and Bridge was almost unknown, we passed the time with simple gambling games like Shoot!, Brag and Pontoon

There had been changes in the Section while I remained on the *Batory* and the only foreign language we now had in common was French. This widened the scope of our speculations, but as yet none of us guessed the truth that the Force was being prepared for landing in Madagascar

More important to me was that one of the French-speaking replacements for those who only spoke Spanish was Maurice Ohana and for the next year I should have a friend in my own Section. Of him I wrote in a later book, since he remains a valued friend to this day—

I went to see another Parisian friend, a Parisian one might almost say by nationality. I do not know what country issues his passport to Maurice Ohana but he belongs integrally to this city. He was born in Casablanca, his parentage a mixture of Gibraltarian, Sefardi-Jewish, Andalucian-Spanish and English. We were in the army together for the first three years of the war—perhaps only Field Security could have brought together two such unlikely comrades-in-arms. Maurice is the only man of whom I have known from the first, with no evidence but my own instincts, that he had genius. This might not be strange if he were a writer, but he was then and is now a composer, and I had no technical knowledge of music. The genius I only sensed has been proved since then, though, and he holds a high if ambiguous position. . . . It was while we were on the *Winchester Castle* on our way to Scapa Flow for one of our endless landing exercises that he composed his first serious piece, *Sarabande*. Hearing of his abilities the OC Troops on the ship which took us out to Madagascar sent for our young FSO and said—"Hear you have a pianist fellow in your Section. Tell him to report to the Officers' Mess tonight to play during dinner." Maurice was furious and at first decided to disobey the order, but had a better idea and shook the dining-saloon with weird discords and cacophony till he was told to desist. "Can't you play anything else?" asked the OC Troops sulkily. "Bit of Mendelssohn or something?" "Sorry, sir," said Maurice. "I only play modern Spanish music." He was dismissed and his place taken by another member of our Section who was a church organist in civil life.

Maurice had the kind of humour which wore well in the army and it was given full scope by the solemn schoolmasters of our Section. I think I have laughed with him more than with any of my friends, and it was with him that I spent those first precious evenings ashore in Durban, eating and drinking lavishly after two years of rationing and army food. After Madagascar we both took commissions and went different ways, Maurice to East Africa and Italy, I to India, but army life never seemed quite so funny again.

Maurice was in demand in the Sergeants' Mess of the *Winchester Castle* as a pianist but suffered because he wanted to entertain but could not improvise the kind of music that was required, and he could only please a few of us. At last he discovered that Chopin's *Etude in E Major* had been adapted for a popular tune known to them all, and in playing the original he did not offend by being too highbrow. Utterly unlike a soldier, not even resembling an Englishman, he was yet a popular man on board. All of us in Field Security were considered a little odd.

The exercise lasted for the last weeks of October and Inverary castle, seen from the ship in all its fairy-story unreality, its little turrets and archways, looked in the autumn mists as though it had been designed by Walt Disney. I went ashore in Inverary and climbed the heathery hills above the loch with Maurice—who protested that he had no use for such pointless exercise—and a couple of artificer apprentices from the ship. An ill-matched but talkative quartet, we ate one of those enormous meals called 'tea' in Scotland with bannocks, oatcakes, scones, shortcake and what-have-you, with jam and even cream, provender to which I was to become accustomed in the months ahead. We might have been peacetime tourists on our way to the Highlands.

Once again I managed to remain on board when the Section went ashore—not in charge of baggage but attached to a company of the Royal Marines, and when I received orders to move it was to Melrose where Divisional Headquarters had been established. I remember enjoying the 200-odd mile solitary cycle ride in early November mists. I was fit as a flea and rode like a boy of seventeen trying out his first motor bike.

CHAPTER SIX

Kelso

[1]

VERY good news awaited me. The Force was scattered among various headquarters from Duns to Hawick, so that our Section was scattered with them. I was to go 'on detachment' to Kelso where a battalion of Royal Marines (afterwards the Marine Commandos) was stationed, and Maurice Ohana was to go with me.

I remained in Kelso for nearly six months and although this period was interrupted by several exercises at sea, it was long enough for Kelso to become one of the towns or villages which I think of as having been my home. Sometimes I have not remained in them long enough to justify the use of the word, but they have had for me certain qualities, or certain associations which make me remember them with a warmth that most people feel only for their birthplace, or the place in which they have passed their married life and brought up their children. They have not always been the city which I have known best in each country—this is intimacy of another kind so that although I have remained for long periods in Paris and have loved it well, it is Erstein in Alsace and Roquefort in the Landes which are my home-towns in France, the village of Monschau not the city of Cologne in Germany, Belgaum rather than Bombay in India, Anivorano not Diego Suarez in Madagascar, Zug in Switzerland, and San Isidro rather than Buenos Aires in Argentina.

These are all abroad and it was the foreign-ness of Kelso which enchanted me as soon as I saw it. Deprived of continental travel for the last three years I saw in the central square of Kelso the *place*, the *platz* of any North European small town, though it particularly resembled parts of Bruges. The inhabitants spoke an unfamiliar tongue and altogether it was like arriving before the war in one of those small undistracting places abroad to which I used to resort for a period to work on a book.

The most acceptable compliment a *sassenach* can pay to the Scots is to find them un-English in character, appearance, customs and speech, and this the lowlanders of Kelso certainly were. I had the feeling that we, the troops, were interrupting a traditional way of life by our presence, that we were strangers in a closed community. The hospitality shown to us was unbounded, the kindness of the inhabitants difficult to exaggerate, but it was given to strangers. We were not made to feel we were interlopers, but we knew that when we had gone Kelso would be unchanged by our stay, would settle down again to life as it had been lived for decades—or, in essentials, for centuries.

It is not to be described as a beautiful place, though its situation on the Tweed is attractive, but it has character, charm and above all a cheerful friendly aspect in spite of the grey stone with which much of it is built.

I was told to find myself a billet for which the Army's allowance was 27s. a week 'all found', an impossibility one would have said, but not in Kelso. I was recommended to try the Queen's Head, a comfortable inn, second only in status to Ednam House which was a three-star hotel. I found Mrs Easson, the proprietress, to be a business-like kindly Scotswoman who agreed to accept me on those terms, an act of notable generosity considering that her *table d'hôte* was quite renowned and she had previously catered for well-to-do people who came here for the fishing.

To say that I was happy in Kelso does not express what I mean. I need to use a modern formula which I dislike in most contexts—it was out of this world. It was unlike anything previously experienced in Civil life, and totally unlike Army life, though it was curiously compounded of both.

I lived as a civilian, allowed to wear civvies 'when necessary for Security work', which meant that I could change into a lounge suit in the evening whenever I wanted, but I was paid, given the use of a motor-cycle, and provided with comfortable quarters and very good food by the Army and the charity of Mrs Easson. I was under Army orders with all that it implied of restricted liberty, but in practice this meant very little and I might have been any guest staying at the Queen's Head. The anomalies of the situation were manifold. Annis would come over from Melrose to pay me—and at my invitation stay to lunch in the hotel. I did what work there was, gave Security lectures to every Company of the Royal Marines and handled any Security matter that arose in the town, but rose at what hour I liked, stayed up all night on occasion, and rode about the countryside at will. Now and again I received typewritten orders from Heacock, like the following.

SUBJECT:- *General Instructions to NCOs.*
A/S/Sgt. Cooke, R.C.

1. Under the provisions of ACI 2361 of 29.11.41 the scales of baggage to be taken overseas has been restricted to the following amounts:-
Officers—4 cwt. WOs—2 cwt. Other Ranks—1 Universal & 1 Sea Kit bag.

This scale will under no circumstances be increased but may be reduced for certain destinations.
FS NCOs will therefore ensure that they do not carry kit in excess of issues or which cannot be contained in the two kit bags allowed. Any additional kit should be sent home immediately as no arrangements can be made for the disposal of such in the event of a move.

2. The following discrepancy appears between your transport work-ticket and the monthly log sheet. You show 11 miles as having been covered on the 18th on one form but 18 miles on the other. It is not understood why the figures had been altered on the log sheet—these were the figures after the workshop inspection and should not have been altered in any way.

But I did not see Heacock for several months and only heard reports of his disapproval of the whole idea of sending us out on detachment.

Yet my life at Kelso differed from that of peacetime in one important respect—I belonged to something bigger than myself. I might wear civvy clothes sometimes and live in comfort, but I was one of the troops in the town and respected their criteria. My friends were among them, my loyalties were to them and I had the comforting reassurance that only comes from being one in a crowd and the relief from all doubts about the future, all nagging ambitions and anxieties. I had what the sign of Gemini, under which I was born, for ever impels me to seek—the best of both worlds.

[2]

When NCOs of the Intelligence Corps were attached to other units they frequently wore the regimental badges of those with whom they worked—as a form of camouflage, I suppose. This presented a special difficulty for me since the Royal Marines were not, of course, a unit of the Army but a Service of their own. Unknown to me Annis put this to the Colonel commanding the battalion stationed at Kelso who said it was a matter for his warrant officers and NCOs to decide, and one of the things —not too plentiful, I hope—of which I boast is that they agreed. I never had the impertinence to wear the globe and laurels but I could have done so. I am proud, too, of the terms on which they accepted me. For the most part their ORs had the naivety and lack of worldly wisdom that came from entering the service as boys and never leaving it in spirit. (I know retired servicemen, today in their fifties and sixties, more guileless than their own children.) I had long ago learned by instinct not to talk down to such men, yet never to be guilty of pretentiousness in speech or manner, to be in fact myself, and

I had the advantage of being a thoroughly common man, in more senses than one. They recognized, however, that I could provide information to settle arguments and supposed I could give advice, even in legal matters. "Hey, Max, you're an educated bastard, what does 'axiomatic' mean?" Or, "I want to talk to you. See, my mother-in-law's been opening her dirty big trap and now my wife writes . . ." Such were the problems with which I was faced. I was not a 'lower deck lawyer'—that was another rather odious type of know-all. But I was expected to use the mysterious power attributed to highly educated people to disentangle the quandaries of the moment. In other respects I was a licensed eccentric, scarcely to be considered as a soldier at all. My rank (staff sergeant) would have been, by virtue of the little crown worn in the arrowhead of stripes, that of colour sergeant in the Royal Marines, and occasionally in moments of extreme formality, I was addressed as 'Colours', but for the most part it was Max, both on board and ashore.

I have met Marines who doubt that there ever was such a thing as a Royal Marine Battalion, and indeed it was unprecedented and soon afterwards became the Royal Marine Commando. It was, I think, the 102nd Battalion which was stationed at Kelso and I came to know scores of those in it by name and nickname. I will not plaster them with flattering adjectives—their service later in the war has been recognized—but say that to a stranger whose attachment to them was itself an unorthodox thing, they seemed the grandest crowd on earth. Or on sea—whichever they were.

I used to meet their officers in a small upstairs bar at the Red Lion and there was nothing of the self-conscious subaltern about them, whatever their rank, that yearning for outward deference from the uncommissioned which afflicted so many. We were all of us, to some extent, playing a part in the services, and it never cost me anything to say 'Sir' to the youngest second-lieutenant—the test was whether a man-to-man relationship could exist under the formalities.

The RSM of the Royals might have been a harder nut to

crack, but whatever he was on parade I found him a delightful fellow to drink with. I was never, in fact, made to feel 'out of it' by any of them.

Soon, as if to balance my 'civilian' relationship with Maurice Ohana and its long intelligent conversations about art and music and books, I made a friend in the battalion, in character as uncomplicated, tough, unpolished, and elemental as I could expect from a young man who had joined the Royal Marines before the war from the poverty of a home in a remote village of County Tyrone. His name, which he was accustomed to give with a sort of amused swagger, was Stewart Hamilton. He was incurably pugnacious, but had physical strength and fighting ability to support him in his all too-frequent manifestations of pugnacity. With this he was inarticulately romantic and responsive to emotion. In speech and manner he exuded the peculiar charm of the Irish, a charm which so beguiles and exasperates Englishmen that they deny its existence, maintaining that 'Irish charm' is a meaningless cliché. He was, in other words, or rather in yet another cliché, a man after my own heart.

He responded to my supposed omniscience and wisdom by attaching himself to me as firmly and loyally as I was attached to his unit. He offered his experience of Service life, his resilience and brute strength, all of which he seemed to think necessary to get me through the hardships and possible dangers of the future, and he relied on what he considered was my superior knowledge of men and things. "Between us we'll conquer the world," he used to say in moments of beer-inspired exultation.

He had peculiar old-soldier relations with a store-keeper about which I did not enquire too closely, though he shared his perqs with me. He had a girl in the town named Margaret, a pretty thoughtful-looking blonde, and he insisted on my acquiring a chirpy little brunette named Mary—for this was his idea of a perfect relationship, two friends each having his own girl to take to dances and sometimes on riverside walks. Against all regulations he would ride on the pillion of my motor-cycle and we explored the countryside, drinking in pubs ten or twenty miles away from headquarters. We became inseparable—a very unorthodox friendship which aroused some comment but no hostility.

With Maurice Ohana my relationship was of a very different kind, though no less important to me. His enchanting French wife used to come and stay with him and had a personality as irresistible as his own. Maurice had billeted himself with the local vet, in a house where there was a piano, and he continued to work undisturbed notwithstanding war and rumours of war. We met every day for coffee, though he would not drink beer with me at night—such an *unspiritual* drink, he said—and never came to the local dances which were held almost nightly in one hall or another throughout that winter. But he delighted in conversation for its own sake, in satire at the expense of the Army, our branch of it, our Section and our CSM. He found Stewart Hamilton droll and unaccountable, as he found most of the British, and treated him with puzzled friendliness.

The girl whose enlacement with me so delighted Stewart was a most attractive child and I adored her whenever I saw her at dances but gave no more thought to her away from them than she gave to me—a warm, caressing, surprisingly possessive relationship on both sides which lasted my stay in Kelso.

The only other friend I had there was Mrs Easson who in the odd terms of bygone slang was 'a brick', 'a good sort', a kind and lovable woman who screened her feelings behind a shrewd Scottish front. She was a woman of instant decisions and firm purpose and we became good friends. This enabled Maurice to say cynically, when asked what I was doing in Kelso, "He's dividing his attention between the proprietress of his hotel, an attractive Scots girl and a beautiful young Marine."

[3]

One of the duties of a Field Security NCO on detachment was

to liaise with the civilian police. The Inspector was a big kindly efficient man who had that peculiar mixture of dourness and twinkling humour which I have found nowhere but in Scotland.

I had been told the name of a 'suspect' in the town, but as usual with the scares and suspicions among civilians in the early war years, the reputation had no foundation. Adam Stempel was, I suppose from the name, of distantly German or Austrian descent and he owned a confectioner's shop and café. Perhaps his father or grandfather had been an immigrant pastrycook who came over in Prince Albert's time, but the man himself spoke nothing but lowland Scots, had never been abroad and was no more a fifth columnist than I had been in Pershore when I was the victim of a similar canard. He was in fact a motherly old person who used to carry cups of hot coffee to Marines on sentry-go and show particular kindness to his favourites when they came to his café.

"I don't think you need worry about Adam Stempel," said the Inspector. "He was thoroughly investigated last year when there was some talk in the town because of his name." Then, with that sly twinkle—"If he's friendly with the troops it has nothing to do with getting information."

This was very true and Stempel's Café became a favourite meeting place. The French who at first find our appetite for breakfast and for that even more idiosyncratic British institution 'coffee and cakes at eleven' frankly incredible, often take to one or the other, and Titine on her visits to Maurice used to join us at Stempel's, but Maurice did not spend as much time there as I did. He was working on what were to be his early compositions and while Stewart and I smoked and talked long over the empty cups he would stand up suddenly and leave us to go back to his billet. I wasted many many hours in that café without a twinge of conscience either as a temporary soldier or as a writer.

On Sundays Adam Stempel would invite a party of Marines, which always included Stewart, who was one of his favourites, to drive in his car to a country club some twenty miles away. It was a hard winter—or perhaps all winters are hard in Roxburghshire?—and I remember driving in icy weather to find the rustic-Ritzy country club where huge log fires awaited us and, as the Marines said, lashings of food and drink.

At night when there was not a dance, we would go to a tavern across the road from the Red Lion to play darts, because the dartboard or the lighting or the atmosphere suited us, and though Stewart was a more erratic player than I was, we would win our beer and go home a trifle muzzily to sleep solidly for nine or ten hours. Proficiency at darts also brought me a rather embarrassing invitation from the Brigadier who wanted to know something of the NCOs from other units attached to the Marines. He seemed a friendly type and made a sporting effort to play at a party he gave for us at headquarters but this kind of deliberate 'mixing' rarely came off in the services, I found. Attempts to ignore rank only ended in an awkward consciousness of it by both sides.

I was playing darts at the pub one night when I received a summons from an Intelligence officer of the Royal Marines to come to the Ednam House Hotel. He met me in the hall and told me that there were three officers of the Pioneer Corps in the bar who were talking so indiscreetly of ships and troop movements that 'something ought to be done about it'. Would I put on civvies, go to the bar, and if I overheard sufficient, take action? This was the kind of job I loathed, but it was after all what I was paid for and I followed instructions.

The talk in the bar was quite astonishing. We heard a lot about 'careless talk' in those days—this surpassed mere carelessness—one could have supposed it was deliberately calculated to reveal as much information as possible, though of course it was nothing of the sort. I sat listening for a time, then realized that there was nothing for it but take the names of the three officers and report them. I had always dreaded this and it was the only occasion, before or after that evening, when I was called on to do it. The three officers, all a little drunk and highly

G

indignant at being asked for their names, said the usual things about the iniquities of the snooper, the unEnglishness of eavesdropping, the innocence of their own behaviour. I was relieved to get back to the public bar a few doors away.

[4]

The news of Pearl Harbour crashed disturbingly into our pleasant life in Kelso but I do not think that we, or the majority of newspaper readers in Britain realized the full significance of it. We had become accustomed to disasters, to the news being so much worse than at first we feared, that these events, happening on the other side of the world between the Americans and the Japanese, had not the cataclysmic horror and fatefulness for us that we should have realized. Besides, whatever the tragedy, they would bring America into the war and sooner or later that would mean victory. Was it selfish to remember this in the critical moment of disaster?

I read the news in my daily paper on a Sunday morning in the quiet breakfast-room of the Queen's Head. It was one of the compensations of Army life that whatever the magnitude of outside events, routine was paramount and heartless optimism was a duty. To this day I have never been able to calculate the deathroll in the Japanese attack or to enumerate the losses in ships and installations—a sort of blindness withheld me from doing so. The Americans, I supposed, with wishful thinking both callous and unintelligent, would soon make good their losses, and whatever the suffering in the meantime, the war would be won. I may have guessed a little of the destruction and casualties yet to come but in the weeks that followed the first shock of Pearl Harbour I was more encouraged than dismayed.

And life went on in Kelso where the length of our stay made the place seem like a garrison town. Snow fell before Christmas, a heavy dry fall which lay solidly on the hills as though it would be there for the rest of the winter. The tramp of Army boots grew muffled as we hurried through the streets on our way to dances or the busy fish-and-chip shop.

Christmas had some meaning in that little continental-seeming snowbound town. It was perhaps Dickensian and sentimental but it was not the shopkeepers' gimmick that it has become, all over Europe, in recent years. I was reminded of a Christmas of three years before which I had spent in Germany rather than the rather sad feast of a year ago at the Winchester depot. The Marines had, as they said, got their feet under the table in scores of Kelso households and were not allowed to feel any of the shortages in civilian life. There was a battalion concert in which a Marine sergeant and I, both wearing dinner-jackets borrowed in the town, impersonated the Western Brothers, writing words which guyed those officers who were familiar figures to us all by reason of their mannerisms or eccentricities of appearance—the sort of licensed buffoonery allowed at this season.

Mrs Easson wanted a Christmas tree for the saloon bar of the Queen's Head and lent me her sports car in order to drive out and find one. Stewart had been issued with a useful piece of equipment called a machete, and armed with this we drove through the snow on a lonely road looking for a suitable plantation. We passed no other vehicle, for petrol was in extremely short supply and only a few farmers or an occasional farm lorry carrying essential supplies were on the road. I remember keeping guard, however, in case anyone should approach while Stewart hacked down a splendid conifer and loaded it into the car. That might have been an excusable theft but when the landlord of the pub in which we played darts offered us a quid for a similar tree, and several others made bids, our consciences must have become a bit ragged. However, as Stewart pointed out, it was Christmas time and a few pounds came in very handy for the expenses of the holiday. "God feeds his sparrows," he said. After that I used the car quite often, for Stewart had a system of ingeniously siphoning WD petrol into its tank.

I had never passed Hogmanay in Scotland and remember a wild and festive night which ended in the central square of the town. There were no church bells, of course, but I think the town clock struck midnight, on which, irrespective of sex or uniform, there was a consensus of promiscuous kissing.

[5]

There was one other occasion during the time I was in Kelso which was memorable to me, though it had not much significance for Stewart, who shared it.

A few miles away was the village of Yetholm or Kirk Yelholm which throughout the last century and during the early years of this one had been famous for its gypsies. I have written about the gypsies of Yetholm in *The Moon in My Pocket* but I want to recall my visit to the place among the most curious incidents of that time.

I rode through the crisp snow on a clear and arctic afternoon, Stewart riding pillion. Once again we passed no traffic and even as we entered the village there was no one in sight. I expected some remnant of the great gypsy tribe of Faa who had travelled and lorded it among the outcasts in Scotland for four hundred years since James V concluded a treaty with 'oure louit Johnne Faa, Lord and Erle of Little Egypt' in 1540, but not even a ghost of the royal scalliwags was to be found. The Faas had been hanged for the offence of 'abyding within the kingdom, they being Egyptianis'; they were the heroes of the old ballad about Jockie Faa and the Countess of Cassilis, they had fought the dreadful Shaws from across the border at the sanguinary gypsy battle of Rommano in Tweeddale in 1677, and one of them, Geordie Faa, the husband of Scott's Meg Merriless, was slain by the gaolbreaker Robert Johnstone.

They had been 'transported to Carolino', and had been hanged for sheep-stealing and for their loyalty to the Stuarts, and at last, at the end of the eighteenth century, the residue of the tribe had settled at Yetholm.

The word 'settled' is ominous, for from that date they began to lose all claim to be considered true Romanies, whose very essence is their nomadic way of life. The first to inhabit the 'gypsy palace' there, a modest cottage on a slope on the outskirts of the village, was called Wull Faa, the Gypsy King, and his son William reigned from 1784 to 1847 and his grand-nephew Charles Blyth from 1847 to 1861, but these were no more than courtesy titles, paraded to attract the attention of the *gorgios* and free drinks at the inn of which Wull Faa was the landlord. The last of them, known as Queen Esther Faa-Blythe, lived until 1883, and drove a donkey cart round the countryside selling pottery.

But if the true Romani strain was lost, as it had been lost all over Great Britain, a great deal of picturesque tradition and myth remained. The little cottage in which the last Faas lived had been called 'the Capital of Upper Egypt', and George Borrow, the first and still the greatest of the Romani Rais (or Romany Ryes as he quaintly spelt it), had visited it in 1861, finding it a show place for the gullible *gorgio* even then. All that was left of the murderous and swaggering Faas, those members of the 'criminal tribes' as they were still called in India where they persist unchanged, was a fable of former greatness among a breed of Scottish muggers and tinkers settled in a village, and now even the last of these had disappeared and Yetholm had as sober a *gorgio* population as you could hope to find. The Faas who had inspired moonshine and fiction, balladry and romance had vanished utterly, and the 'palace' of their successors was inhabited by a farm worker and his family who had never heard of the gypsies.

But the inn remained, modernized perhaps from what it was when Borrow came to it eighty years earlier, but in essentials unchanged. "It is still an inn", Borrow was told by a villager, "and always been an inn; and though it has an eerie look it is sometimes lively enough, more especially after the Gypsies have returned from their summer excursions in the country. It's a roaring place then. They spend most of their sleight-o'-hand gains in that house."

Moreover it was open, and Stewart and I went in from the icy cold and hugged the fire from a wooden settle. The landlord was friendly but could tell us nothing of the gypsies—as far as he knew there was not one in the place and had not been in recent memory. However, he pointed out the 'palace' in all its modesty and we left the fire to take some pictures, then returned to eat and drink before facing the darkening road between here and Kelso.

CHAPTER SEVEN

Barra

[1]

COMPTON MACKENZIE wrote and invited me to spend a leave
with him on the Isle of Barra and something I had long wanted
to do became suddenly possible. I have told in *The Sound of
Revelry* how in boyhood I had only one kind of hero-worship,
that for writers, ancient and modern. Generals, statesmen,
warrior kings, painters—you could have the lot in exchange for
Villon, say, or Byron or vindictive little Pope, or Chris
Marlowe daring to defy all right-minded opinion, or others who
worked or drank themselves to death for the sake of getting
their precious words down on paper. I made heroes of men
whose lives were as disparate as Fielding and Tennyson but as I
see now there was usually something in their biography as well
as in their work which appealed to my biased romanticism. The
living example of this was Compton Mackenzie. I believed that
Sinister Street was a truly great novel and I had watched its
author, through accounts published in newspapers or books,
on his picturesque progress from an undergraduate of somewhat startling achievements, to his notable part in the First
World War, his spectacular stay in Capri, his adoption of
island homes, his championship of the cause of Edward VIII
against—as I choose to see it—Stanley Baldwin and the
Archbishop of Canterbury, his prosecution at the Old Bailey
for a supposed breach of Security in a book published nearly
twenty years after the events described, his espousal of romantic
causes like Scottish Nationalism, his full, varied and eventful
life. Modern writers, I thought, had been dreary and in-

dustrious—not only their books but their lives were dull, at least to the onlooker, but here was one who had both written and lived with panache. Then, a year before the outbreak of war, I had met him and found that he lived up to my somewhat high-falutin conception. I did not know then of the distorted views he so uncharacteristically holds of Bosie Douglas and Robert Ross, but it would not have qualified my admiration then, as it has not done since.

When his letter and later his telegram came I felt that the whole prospect took on the colour of adventure. Although it was not admitted by the authorities, the leave that was being granted to us now was embarkation leave and to travel at the Army's expense—for we could choose whatever destination we liked for leave—to the Outer Hebrides and meet Monty Mackenzie on his own ground and listen, sitting by his own fireside, to one of the most brilliant conversationalists since the eighteenth century, was about all I wanted. Besides, though I was happy in the deliberately sought philistinism of Army life and the undemanding company of men like Stewart and his friends, and although I had put away writing materials for the duration of war, it would be gratifying for a time to be in a civilized and—odious but inevitable word—cultured home.

There was no difficulty about obtaining a pass, though there cannot have been many in the Force who demanded to go by ship to the Outer Hebrides for their leave, and I had one of the roughest passages I have ever suffered, stretched on hard boards in the third-class quarters of a small packet steamer. Even this had to be abandoned late at night for the even smaller and more convulsive boat that ran to Barra.

I waited several hours for this in some Hebridean port whose name and situation I cannot remember. There was a hotel whose proprietor was a friend of Monty's and had been warned of my coming and I ate and drank whisky by a roaring log fire till some time long past midnight when I went on board the Barra ferry. I eventually came ashore just before dawn and was met by Monty's chauffeur, a Highlander named Kenny

MacCormick whose story is told in Mackenzie's *My Life and Times*.

I remember that stormy arrival well and how I entered the kitchen of Suidheachan to come on the unusual spectacle of five gigantic Siamese cats sleeping on top of the Aga cooker. A last whisky and I slept till noon.

[2]

Chrissie MacSween, then Monty's secretary and later his second wife, ran his house for him and realized very fully what were the material wants of a temporary soldier coming on leave —breakfast in bed, an hour with the newspaper before getting up, lots of food and drink and above all freedom to be as lazy as one liked. She did not say, 'You ought to get some exercise, you know'; she did not recommend the beauties of Barra or the advantages of a little run in the car to see them. She did not even talk about 'getting some fresh air' or 'meeting interesting people'. She simply encouraged me to do what I wanted all day, and what I wanted was to 'sit about doing nothing' until Monty made an appearance some time in the afternoon or early evening. Thereafter we talked till the small hours of the morning. I left the house only twice—to take some photographs of Monty in his Home Guard uniform, wearing the kilt and a variety of medal ribbons, Greek as well as British, and to go to Mass on Sunday with his niece. I saw nothing of Barra except the quay on the night of arrival and the morning of departure, I met none of the neighbours except the RAF officers in charge of a detachment on the island, and I wanted no variation. I had rarely been happier.

On the first evening when drinking whisky at dinner, as Monty frequently did, I thought there was some quality, a particular blandness and charm about that whisky, and remarked on it.

"God in His mercy looked down," said Monty parenthetically but with a twinkle, "on these little islands which had never changed their Faith and when a ship had to be wrecked with a cargo of the finest Scotch on its way to safe-keeping in the United States, He saw to it that this happened hereabouts. You are drinking some of that whisky."

Ten years later I read the full story and saw the film of *Whisky Galore,* with Monty playing the ship's captain as Hugh Walpole had once played a preacher in a film of his novel *The Cathedral.* It appeared in America under the title *Tight Little Island* in revenge perhaps for the inept title forced on *Sinister Street* in its American edition—*Youth's Encounter.*

I understood Monty's reference to 'islands which had never changed their faith' better when I went to Mass on Sunday and heard a sermon preached in Gaelic in the parish church which was Catholic. I had never realized that Protestantism had not reached so far as the Outer Hebrides during the Reformation, or that although it made some progress in the centuries afterwards the Islands are still in the care of the Church.

Monty also told me the story of Kenny MacCormick and the Home Guard with rather more crackle than he chose to give it more than twenty years later when he came to write it in *My Life and Times.* Monty was in command of the Home Guard on Barra, a duty he took seriously. His only means of getting about the island and of communicating with the men in his command was through Kenny, who spoke Gaelic and drove his car, and Kenny was threatened by the call-up of men in his age group. Monty was determined to obtain his exemption on these grounds and had written to the authorities on the mainland stating his case. The correspondence had grown, as correspondence with War Office offshoots was apt to do, into prolixity on their side and bluntness on Monty's, and at last the authorities had threatened to enforce their determination to conscript Kenny. Monty had relied, characteristically, that should anyone arrive on the island with the intention of carrying out this threat, as commanding officer of the only military force on Barra he would take into custody such persons and return them under arrest to the mainland. There, for the moment, the matter rested.

Monty was enjoying it.

"Every now and again in my life I have had to force a sudden uproar in the newspapers. First there was the banning of *Sinister Street* by the lending libraries, then the prosecution at the Old Bailey, then the noise about *The Windsor Tapestry* and the *Sunday Pictorial*. This is going to be another."

There seems little doubt that it would have been if Monty had carried out his threat. Kenny, however, was called up.

[3]

The house, as I remember it, was single-storied but covered a wide area of grassland overlooking the Atlantic. The largest room was the library and it had one of those startling landscape windows which can only be made successfully in a room over-looking the sea. One saw what appeared to be a water-colour painted in vivid tints, framed realistically and depicting a sandy beach with breakers rolling in sunlight. But as one looked more closely one saw that the breakers were rolling in fact and one realized that one was looking through glass on the Atlantic.

I spent much time in the library, not so much in reading as in looking through the press-cutting albums which went back to reviews of Monty's first poems and recorded in headlines the tumult and shouting over the lending library ban on *Sinister Street* and Monty's other early adventures in public relations. There was one book which belonged to Faith, his wife, which I think was perhaps the most enviable bibliographical curiosity I had seen. It was a copy of *Vestal Fire* which some critics consider his most perfect novel, extra-illustrated with photographs of the real characters depicted, or partly depicted, in the novel. Here were Marsac-Langerstrom (Jacques Adelsward-Fersen), Virginia and Mamie Pepworth-Norton (Kate and Sadie Wolcott-Perry), Carlo (Nino Cesarini) and the rest, and some of the houses in which they lived.

In that connection I made one of those odd discoveries about Monty's work which has not, I think, been otherwise noted. I did much the same thing with John Galsworthy when I pointed out to him that several sections of the *Forsyte Saga* and half a dozen short stories ended with a line of blank verse which sometimes became manneristic—'and in the air the scent of fallen leaves', 'and in young Jolyon's face he slammed the door'. Galsworthy did not thank me for that, though he recognized, for the first time, the truth of it. Monty laughed over his and admitted it; it was that the Pepworth-Nortons, the adorable old ladies of Sirene who had joined their two names in one, had already appeared in very different surroundings in Hampshire in *Sylvia Scarlett* as the Miss Horne and Miss Hobart, with much the same characteristics, though in a humbler way. I probably knew, and know to this day, as much about Monty's work as anyone living, not excluding himself who is notoriously forgetful about it. Who else remembers every detail of his vast trilogy of novels about a parson's life and eventual conversion? Who knows his *Kensington Rhymes,* the book of *Poems* he wrote while still at Oxford, the childrens books, and all the *Winds of Love,* as well as the comedies from *Poor Relations* to the latest adventure of the *Monarch of the Glen*? Only some earnest student writing a thesis perhaps, but for me they have been part of my sentient life.

[4]

It is difficult to give the flavour of a man's conversation, however distinctive. One may reproduce anecdotes and witticisms, may describe the tone of voice and the gestures, but none of these makes the essence of genius in talk—a very different thing from genius in writing. I knew this when long before I came to Barra I had heard Bosie Douglas try to tell me about the conversation of Oscar Wilde at his best. Bosie had achieved only words like 'brilliant' and 'charming' and paradoxically 'memorable', though he, better than anyone, knew what it was like to listen to Oscar not only in his prime but in Paris at the last.

I suppose there are great conversationalists today; except for Monty Mackenzie I have not heard them, though I have known and listened respectfully to some considered masters. Joad was too dogmatic, Coward too irrepressibly scintillating for depth, Bob Boothby too temperamentally indolent and Beverley Nichols too flippant. Monty had everything; he could discuss a point of serious literary criticism without being a bore, he could drop into superb mimicry, a hereditary gift perhaps, he could be hilariously funny without the heavy-handed malice which is a characteristic of much modern conversation, or vividly reminiscent. His range was immense, with a telling knowledge of period and touches of startling actuality. He had —what many of us lack, I sadly recognize—a sense of compassion which never let him score the easy victories of spite and allowed him the more genial effects that came from a gift for ridicule.

He was particularly entertaining on his contemporary writers, Hugh Walpole, Francis Brett-Young, D. H. Lawrence, Norman Douglas, but several of the set pieces in his firework display were dedicated to Henry James and Hall Caine.

Some of the stories he told me at that time have appeared in *My Life and Times*, but not, I choose to believe, with quite the verve of the speaking voice. The art of the raconteur dies with him, whatever recordings may have been made, for it owes something to the listener, to the occasion, perhaps to the provocation, and it loses even more in the written version. You may read Monty's stories of D. H. Lawrence, they may even be recorded, but nothing can compensate for the physical presence of the narrator, the mimicry with which he reproduced the voice with its gentle North Country accent and the elfin glee with which he told them, not as a rehearsed effort but as a natural part of a long conversation. To hear Monty quoting—'There won't be another war. *I* won't allow it,' at the end of one of poor Lawrence's egomaniac tirades was not only brilliant comedy but also valuable criticism on the man and his work which some of his more idolatrous worshippers might well study.

More hilarious, perhaps, was another story told in *My Life and Times* of that nearly incredible character Hall Caine taking Edward VII on a tour of the Isle of Man. From being, as Monty said, Dante Gabriel Rossetti's valet, Hall Caine had risen by laudable persistence and industry to stardom as a writer of best sellers, complete with silver hair trained like that in a Shakespearean monument about his bald dome, and wearing a broad-brimmed black hat and Thespian cloak. He posed as the Manx Wizard, only matched both in his pretensions and the sales of his book by Marie Corelli, who kept up much the same sort of pantomine in Stratford-on-Avon. Monty had been summoned as a very young man by Hall Caine for some sort of conference connected with the theatre and it was a good thing for us that he was, for it inspired one of his superbly comic impersonations.

Francis Brett Young, of whom Monty was sincerely fond, gave him two more stories, one of which he has told in print—('Surely, Monty, you are not implying that I have no sense of humour?') The other he has not seen fit to recall and I shall respect his reticence. He was perhaps at his best in talking about Hugh Walpole, Hughie as he always called him, because the mixture of absurdity and likeableness in Walpole was irresistible to him.

But it was not only in narrative, however sublimely comic or evocative, that he passed those midnight hours—he had wide sympathies and wisdom which he gave as readily to his hearers as entertainment. He could question searchingly and give pithy advice; he could bring out the best in one and treat

it with respect. He made me realize that the war would not last
for ever—a difficult realization for a serviceman who had accepted his lot as perennial. He reminded me that the time for
writing books and living ambitiously would come again for
me, that I should not always be able to luxuriate in the unthinking society of the Army. All in all I think now that if I
gained nothing as a reward for those months of training in
Combined Operations but a leave pass to Barra, they were
worth it.

[5]

There was a legacy or bonus from that leave with Monty
Mackenzie for he wrote to his friends the Maxwell Scotts at
Abbotsford and they invited me over for the day.

This too might have been the realization of an early ambition if it had come twenty years earlier, when I read, seriatim,
every novel of Sir Walter Scott and swore that nothing should
tempt me from allegiance to his memory. I understand that in
this debunking age memory has become a little tarnished and
the heroic industry with which Scott toiled to pay off his
publishers' debts is not considered such a selfless sacrifice as it
once seemed, nor his behaviour in money matters so impec-
cably disinterested. But the portrait satisfied me once of an
unworldly generous man who gave himself not to the creation
and maintenance of his Gothic and grandiose home but to the
voluntary repayment of the small investors who had trusted
him. His works too have suffered from a continuous and steep
decline in popular favour since Victorian times, when countless
editions of the Waverley Novels were printed and no literate
home was considered furnished without one of them. In spite of
recent attempts to revive interest, few people feel that the
pleasurable and leisurely reading of Scott is a necessary part of
education. He has become an author to read 'some day, when I

have time', and neither the cinema nor television has done much to exploit his wonderful potentialities. (Perhaps script-writers are intimidated by the great mass of verbiage round his themes?) Only those who like 'to lose themselves in a good book,' and a few artful academic critics remain true addicts.

I knew all about Abbotsford as a literary shrine and it seemed to me piquant and curious that in the middle of a war, escaping from military duties for a day, I should be asked to lunch there with its creator's descendants. That I should be a sergeant lunching with a major-general had its own oddity, though of a more conventional kind. But it all became serenely natural and easy. The General was Zone Commander of the Scottish Border Home Guard but never mentioned military matters and Lady Maxwell Scott was a vivacious Frenchwoman who detested de Gaulle, and they both spoke of Monty Macken-zie as 'a young man', which in a sense he was, and is today in his eighties. The General showed me Scott's crowded little study and the 'secret' staircase to his bedroom built so that he could work all night and crawl to bed for a time without disturbing the household.

[6]

There was a last Exercise before we embarked, the most realistic of them all, for although we did not know it at the time, the conditions of landing and moving overland were planned to be exactly as we should find them in Madagascar, intense cold serving for intense heat. It took place in the Orkneys to which we were transported in the now familiar ships earmarked for Combined Operations and I was on the *Winchester Castle* again.

We landed in a blizzard and the whole exercise took place in driving snow and intense cold. I found the lonely cottage of a crofter whose wife gave shelter to the Section for the night and we slept on beds like the bunks of a cabin and wondered whether a Combined Operation had been planned for Iceland or Norway.

Back on board next day we lay off Kirkwall and it was here I overheard a scrap of conversation between two Marines who were leaning thoughtfully over the rail of the ship.

"Ah fook'n did."

"You fook'n didn't."

"Ah fook'n *did*!"

"*You* fook'n didn't!"

"*Ah fook'n did*!"

"Oh fook off for fook's sake!"

It was here, also, that I heard a story from one of the Royals which earned me a night ashore in Kirkwall after the exercise was over. He had seen a man taking photographs. He had actually watched (and had two witnesses to prove it), a man openly taking photographs, probably with a Leica, of military operations! This it may be remembered was considered almost a capital offence at that time—sufficiently serious anyhow to justify an immediate investigation ashore. The convoy would not sail till next day so I managed to persuade Annis to obtain authority for me, with the Marine who had seen the photographer, to be put ashore.

As usual, the offence turned out to be an empty scare. There was a Field Security Section permanently stationed in the Orkneys and they identified the offender as an enthusiast who kept a photographer's shop in the town, an inoffensive character who had no idea that it was forbidden to take pictures of troops. He should be warned and there the matter ended, but a night at the local inn at Kirkwall, with good darts and food and beer, was for some reason, not easily recognizable now, a tremendous treat, a coveted privilege secured by praiseworthy contrivance, and both the Marine and I were greatly envied.

The Royal Marines, however, were not to be used for the Madagascar landings and a week later I said goodbye to them

H

and to Kelso and reported at headquarters. We were to embark
with our motor cycles at Gourock and although the orders were
the same as on previous occasions which had led to nothing,
there was an air of finality about this and nobody for a moment
doubted that it was to be 'the real thing' at last.

CHAPTER EIGHT

Atlantic

[1]

ON the way to Gourock I was attacked by influenza, an old enemy of mine which strikes once or twice every winter. Long custom has taught me exactly how to treat it—a warm bed and a couple of aspirin to take down the temperature which sometimes rises to 103, then a few days' rest and I am as good as new, but the only part of this simple treatment obtainable while motor cycling across Scotland in a chilly rainstorm was the aspirin and I reached Gourock in a raging fever. When, after the usual delay, I went on board I collapsed and was taken to the sick bay.

It was three or four days before I became more than cursorily conscious of my surroundings and then through information supplied by the sick bay orderly, a young Glaswegian. I was on a troopship named *Keren,* for the first time under the White Ensign. *Keren* was part of the largest convoy to leave a British port during the Second World War. She appeared to be heading in a southerly direction and there had already been a submarine alert, with action stations and life-jackets, while I had been comfortably sleeping off my fever. On board was a battalion of Royal Scots Fusiliers of whom my informant was one, also a Field Battery and a few odds and sods including some of my Section. I knew that the RSFs were part of 21st Independent Brigade and had been training Combined Operations but I had never fallen in with them during training.

A fuller realization of all this brought some curious apprehensions, dulled by my recumbent condition and the inertia which followed my fever. Suppose there should be another submarine alert or, less credibly, an attack? There would be lifeboats, I comfortably assured myself, for all on board, but what provision, if any, would be made for those in the sick bay unable to reach them or do anything else? It seems to me, as I recall it, a real and dangerous contingency but at the time it was made remote by those who shared it, the MO and the sick bay orderlies who behaved as though it did not exist. What was important was the food supplied to us, the rumours that reached us about our eventual destination, the news that as a sergeant I should be in the Petty Officers' Mess and receive my daily tot of rum. The fact that this was a vast convoy, 'butting through the Channel in the mad March days', of which *Keren* with a mere battalion on board, was an insignificant component, in which the whole Brigade of which we were a part filled only half a dozen troopships, while many more would round the Cape of Good Hope bound for the Suez and North Africa; none of this would have meant much to me just then, even if I had been aware of it. I slept and ate, and when there was in fact another submarine alert, and the orderlies were forced to appear in life-jackets, I indulged in sleepy fatalism and felt that if anything unpleasant should occur I would be 'rocked in the cradle of the deep', a placid form of death as everyone had always told me.

But nothing unpleasant did occur, and the weeks following that rest in the sick bay (during which we took a course—some said, no one knowing—almost to the coast of South America) were some of the best, if outwardly most uneventful, of my whole time in the Army.

Why? It was the real thing at last, we were going somewhere not just on an exercise. This voyage would have a reason and an objective and should test my capacity for—adventure, if you must know. For at thirty-nine years old, after several attempts in civilian life to find and follow a plausibly romantic star, after wandering improvidently to places remote in geography and spirit from my middle-class upbringing, after travelling with a circus and living with gypsies and spurning the stay-at-home necessities of a writer's existence, preferring the people I met in tents and living-waggons to intellectuals or my fellow writers, after cultivating my defiance of the class in which I was born and the standards I had inherited from my parents, I had at last, on this ship and on this voyage, found what all along I had craved, consciously or not, a chance to prove myself. It was not my courage I was testing, it was my sincerity. If I had really longed above all else to be a common man, to overcome the temptations of intellect and the pleasures of the contemplative life, now was the time to do it. It has been easy to escape a social ambience in which I could never have been anything but an odd man out, but how far had it been an honest preference for the a-social? Had I really been free from snobbishness or merely an inverted snob, boasting of my sympathy with out-casts? I believed that I preferred playing darts in a public bar to dining out or meeting on equal terms the distinguished and the famous, but as I had not had any frequent opportunities for the last-named, how far had the preference been cultivated by necessity? How much of it was real? I believed myself to be a good mixer, apt to be given the confidence of the scarcely articulate and at the same time able to join in the counsels of the eminent. How good or how vain would this claim prove? On this ship and among these men I should soon discover.

For this was what I had expected to find when I joined the Army. The Royal Scots Fusiliers were very different from the Royal Marines and not only because they were infantrymen and not a *corps élite*. They had been in India for a long and gruelling tour of duty and had in fact only been brought home from the East in recent months. Almost all of them were regular soldiers in the sense that all but the youngest had been re-cruited before the outbreak of war. They bore far more resemblance to the soldiers of Kipling than to members of the conscript Army of that time. They came from the Gorbals or other grim areas of Clydeside and most of them had joined to relieve the stress of penury in their homes in the workless years. They were tough as old boots, having the very qualities of hardworn leather. They gambled every penny of their ship-board pay and sometimes fought over their gambling. The only difference between the Fusiliers, packed to sweat on troopdecks, and the sergeants, among whom my lot was more generally thrown, was that the sergeants had been in the Regiment longer and learned a certain amount of discretion and knew discipline both in authority and obedience. They had not much respect for most of their officers, except for their CO, a Colonel Armstrong, who induced them to march round the decks in full kit for hours on end to prepare for our landings by leading them in that monotonous fatigue himself, though he was a man approaching fifty.

In conversation they were consistently bawdy and violent except when at a touch they became interested in something foreign to their own experience or appealing to their concealed sentiments. Then they were almost childlike in their demands for more information. Many of them belonged to the semi-criminal classes of pre-war Glasgow, where petty crime was fought by more brutal methods than today. Men of other units on board had been advised to buy those metal D-shaped locks with padlocks to guard their kitbags in the hold of the ship, and on arrival in Durban discovered that a raiding party had got into the hold with a cut-throat razor, had neatly removed the top of all the kitbags so secured and rifled them, supposing that locked kitbags would be the only ones containing anything of value. (I was lucky; I did not have a padlock.)

But gambling, more than theft or buggery, was their ship-board vice. Fusiliers were paid ten shillings a week on board, the rest of their meagre wages going to their credit, but distribution of ten shillings meant countless schools of Nap, dwindling before the end of the week to one or two schools in which the whole Battalion's pay was concentrated, and finally to one rich school like the high table at Monte Carlo with piles of notes before each player. Men would momentarily control a hundred pounds or more and one of them was reputed to have walked off the ship at Durban a rich man.

They were aggressively sentimental and it took only a casual enquiry to bring a wallet full of photographs from the pocket of an Army-hardened Fusilier. 'That's the wife. Those are my two kids.' They did not distrust what they took to be superior education in others—on the contrary they were inclined to exploit it to relieve the boredom of the long voyage by conversation.

But they were, as they would prove during their brief engagement with the Vichy French in Madagascar, wholly without fear and in the hardships they suffered during our six months on the island gifted with endurance, humour and courage.

[2]

Another thing about that voyage that made it remarkable was the fact that throughout its four or five—or was it even more?—weeks, we were without the physical presence of women. Women were in our thoughts, in our talk, even perhaps in our prayers; they received most of the letters we wrote, inspired the plans which we were for ever making for 'after the war' and may have restrained some of our lewder impulses. But they were not there—at any rate on any of the ships which carried the Force intended for Madagascar, since no nurses, no members of any of the women's Services and of course no civilian women were on board. For the great majority of us this was the first and probably the last time that we found ourselves in an entirely womanless world. It was a unique experience, for some scarcely endurable, for others undistinguished among the varied experiences of war, for a few of us intensely interesting.

Away from women, the men behaved in a way perceptibly foreign to their normal existence. Perhaps they had to find compensating qualities in themselves and so became more tender and sentimental with one another, more gentle and understanding. They listened to bores and egotists with less impatience, they suffered hardships and privations with even cruder grumbling than at other times, but with less, far less, real embitterment. They voiced ideas which as comfortably married men they would not have admitted, and claimed ambitions altogether new to them. They developed a sensitiveness that their own wives would scarcely have recognized and a concern for others, especially those in trouble, which united them. The old idea that homosexuality—whatever the meaning of that exasperating word—thrives on segregation of the sexes is nonsense, I think, or at least a gross exaggeration, but indirectly it may be created by men's increased awareness of the attractions of their own rough characters and bodies judged by their own and not women's standards. When I remember my own extraordinary happiness during that voyage I reject the suggestion that it came directly from any such cause but I am sure that I was fortunate enough to have a special appreciation for the qualities of an all-male community, and a special response to its appeal. If that makes me a homosexual then I accept the term in spite of its silliness and ugliness.

Both humour and emotion were uninhibited, and gambling became a dominant interest when there was no loss that would not be repaired by next week's pay-day and no possibility of increasing the allotment of earnings to home needs. We drank our tots of rum and became genial and imaginative with it; we ate better and in better conditions than ashore, we cursed or derided our officers, we were crude in our speech but not in our manners, for a certain fastidiousness is formed in self-protection by communities like ours, we laughed readily at the anomalies of our condition, and old enmities amongst us became cause for more laughter, sometimes merciless. Butts became favourites, and to jesters all things were forgiven. There was a sense of permanence about that shipboard life as though its changeless days would continue and no destination ever be reached.

[3]

When I came out of the sick bay we must have been moving southward, somewhere in the Atlantic. The sea was calm, as it would remain throughout the voyage and the days were passed in breezy sunlight.

I found the Petty Officers' Mess in which there was no fusion but no antagonism between the Services and in the days that followed made the acquaintance, in that sidelong way in which men come together with nothing to introduce them but circumstance, with the RSF Sergeants and those of the RTR and a Field Battery of Gunners who wore flashes of the Light Artillery.

The rum issue was a ceremonial and splendid occasion, on which we enjoyed one of the privileges of the Royal Navy. As I write this (August 1, 1970) I read that it has been withdrawn and groan at the unimaginative stupidity that has ordered this, but groan still more at the pusillanimity of present-day naval men who have, it seems, accepted the loss without effective protest. In an era of protest for sometimes trivial reasons, surely they could have found means to make the Admiralty or the Government or what-have-you aware of their disgust? If the Royal Navy survives the loss as anything more than a Coast Guard service without tradition or romantic orthodoxy, the sailor of the future will feel, and doubtless express, no small contempt for the men who have allowed it to happen.

However, this was 1942 and the rum ration was given not only to the naval personnel on board but to the Army who were in a sense their guests, 'neaters' to us in the PO's Mess and 'two and one' to the rest of the ORs. For a benign half-hour we felt its warmth and inspiration invest our whole beings, and if the imagination was not touched by the idea of Nelson's Blood, the most stolid among us could know its splendid influence. We felt we were heroes, treated as heroes, and had left our commonplace lives behind on land.

There was, as I have said, little fraternization between the

petty officers and sergeants in the Mess; the Navy had its ways
of filling the hours of recreation and we, with less experience of
this life, were tyros who had to learn what the order 'Make and
Mend', piped over the ship's wireless, portended. It must have
been after receiving the rum ration that I challenged a petty
officer, the undisputed darts champion of the ship, to a match—
'best of three legs, 301 up, start and finish on a double'. Darts
was the only game in which I had ever come anywhere near to
excelling and this had stood me in good stead in a wide divers-
ity of occasions. The stake was a pound, an unheard-of sum in
our circumstances, but the betting on both of us was heavy,
which made the occasion tense and my responsibility a grave
one.

Darts is above all a game of confidence and the PO began
with all of it. He started with the first dart and before I had
achieved my initial double, he wanted double-top to finish.
Moreover he got it. It was not confidence but desperation that
enabled me to win the other two legs and the match, while his
own sureness faltered. Over nearly thirty years the details of
the game return to me and I remember now with an ironic
twist of the mind that it was played as we steamed steadily into
the South Atlantic sunlight while behind us the first Russian
counter-offensive in a hideous war was exhausting itself. But
what could have been more important than the collection of my
pound and the handing over of the half-crowns which had
backed me?

There were a few disadvantages in being under the White
Ensign. The ship's Adjutant whom I had known in civil life
asked me to give a lecture to the officers. "Anything that you
think might be interesting. Literature, perhaps, or the circus,"
he suggested airily. "It's a long voyage and everyone wants a
little entertainment." This was understandable and I did not
mind trying to provide it, but I made one condition.

"I want a fee," I said, "of two double Scotches. Paid on the
nail." For rum, magnificently potent as it was, had in time a
certain monotony.

"You shall have it," said the ship's Adjutant and on that assurance I gave the lecture. It was not very difficult to entertain—entertainment was stressed—a group of Navy and Army officers two weeks out from home with nothing to vary their lives. I gave them some literary gossip and a few scandalous anecdotes of contemporary writers, and they ate it. There was applause and kind, if patronizing, comment.

"And now," I said, perhaps a little eagerly. "What about my Scotch?"

This produced a certain discomfort and a tendency to break up the group who had surrounded me while I talked.

"You see, old man . . ." I had become 'old man' for this classless occasion. "It's rather awkward. The Army has to conform to naval rules. It is absolutely forbidden for ORs to enter the Wardroom."

"Do you mean . . ." I began indignantly.

"We're terribly sorry about it. You know what tradition is like in the Royal Navy."

"But it was an agreement. An undertaking. I've fulfilled my part."

"You must see how we're placed. We would like *of course* to stand you a drink, but . . ."

"Its not a matter of standing me a drink. These were the terms of a contract."

I was suddenly conscious of being that nuisance to everybody else in the world, a man who demands his rights. I went back to my own mess deck and never had my Scotch. Since then, like most writers, I have suffered from the non-compliance of others with the agreements they have made; three publishers have gone bankrupt on me, three periodicals by which I was owed money have folded up without paying their contributors and I have lost money I have earned in several ways, but none of them has seemed at the time or since such a gross betrayal of good faith. I *never had my Scotch,* or even, as I said to my friends with more four-letter words than D. H. Lawrence could assemble in a whole book, a sniff of it.

[4]

We called at Freetown, but no one was allowed ashore except some FS men from another ship who were sent to bring the mail abroad. We lay off shore for a whole night while Freetown was visible as a misty shape dimly illuminated like a Malayan village in a novel by Joseph Conrad.

After that there was nothing but the Atlantic for many days of bland and beautiful sunlight. Phosphorus shimmered round the ship at night and flying-fish in shoals leapt by in the long afternoons and reminded me of my first long voyage to South America twenty years before, a voyage with which the present one had many affinities. *Keren* had been a passenger ship in peacetime and someone discovered a set of those absurd wooden race-horses worked by strings which enabled us— officers and senior NCOs only, 'There simply isn't room for more, you see'—to hold make-believe race meetings. Then the RSFs produced kilts for a dozen dancers who took their reels seriously.

We were fairly quiet at night but the officers, whose bar remained open till midnight, occasionally disturbed the peace of the ship to be admonished by furious shouts of 'Shut up you noisy bastards!' from below. 'All right,' I remember thinking, 'I'm going to get a commission just to travel home in comfort and drink whisky as often as I please.' Alas, by the time I came home with my captaincy all ships were dry and I had the most uncomfortable passage I have ever known.

There was a certain hour just before nightfall when I used to go out on a small deck, the lower well-deck aft I think it was called, to watch the rays of the sunset and talk to the friends I had made on board. The Atlantic had not disappeared from view but was insistent and restless about us, and in the breeze of evening the dramatic seascape stirred curious emotions. It was an hour for confidences and the hearing of plans for the future, for a kind of spiritual proximity to others who were touched by it, of comradeship becoming almost articulate in the darkening intimacy. I used to come in from that hour to the lights of the POs' Mess and feel the release from all nervous tension which gambling games provided, I would play 'Shoot!' or 'Ha'penny Brag' till past midnight.

[5]

As a battalion recruited from Clydeside the RSFs had two chaplains, Father McDonnell and a Presbyterian, a younger man whose name I forget, or did not know. Father McDonnell was a sandy-haired thin-lipped man who fought jealously for his flock, engaging in conflict with company commanders who failed to release men from other duties to attend Confession or Mass. He was almost a martinet also with his own congregation of soldiers, and most of them would rather have been absent from parade than admit to their chaplain that they had omitted their religious duties. The Presbyterian was tall and rather serious-looking, thinning over the temples and having a confidential air.

No story of their antagonism reached me on the ship but since these were the days before projects of Reunion became popular, there would have been no shame in at least as much rivalry as between Mr Bennett and Father Victor in *Kim*.

But in Madagascar a few weeks later that antagonism broke out in an episode which led to such hostility that their mutual obligations to forgive must have been sorely tested. In a grubby town named Brickaville near Tamatave the village priest had decamped with the retreating Vichy French, and since a company of RSFs were billetted in the town in very poor accommodation, mostly native huts, what more logical than that the Presbyterian chaplain should have been given the priest's empty house?

I was walking up the dusty street when I heard the Protestant padre's gentle voice inviting me to have a glass of wine.

I had not tasted such a thing since Durban—the only drink left by our blockade of the island being Reunion rum of poor quality which I used to drink with coconut milk.

"A glass of *wine*, Padre? Do you mean it?"

"Come along and I'll show you. I found a cask in the cellar. I don't drink it myself but I don't see why you should not, within reason, enjoy the spoils of war."

"Certainly not," I agreed and we entered his modest quarters.

But the wine which was excellent made me feel uncomfortable, for whether he knew it or not it was Altar wine which the French priest had probably brought to his house for safe-keeping. To do him justice the Presbyterian was a temperance man with little or no experience of vintages and had failed to recognize what he had found. He was keen on good-fellowship and was offering it in the cause of it.

"Like it?" he smiled.

I thanked him and made an excuse to leave.

But when I returned to Brickaville a few weeks later the Company had moved and another had taken its place and Father McDonnell was installed in the priest's house. His indignation could scarcely be controlled. "Do you know what that . . ." He did not use the word which most readily comes to mind, but I think he was uncharitable enough to say 'black-guard' . . . "has done?" And he told me. One would have thought the wine had been already consecrated from the way he spoke of it. I did not tell him that I had had a glass.

But on our voyage out I saw Father McDonnell only at Mass, and the Presbyterian padre only because, he said, he liked to talk sometimes with 'educated men'.

[6]

When we were approaching Durban we still had not been given any official information about our objective, and

Madagascar was only one of the theories we held. So we would go ashore without any precise information to disseminate. But there was need for Security all the same and in those last days I was able to achieve what I at least believed was one of the few— if not the only—thoroughly useful acts during my whole time in the 'I' Corps. If words, in that sense, are ever as useful as we hope. I was told to broadcast, over the ship's radio, a talk on Security of Information.

I had broadcast fairly often for the BBC from its early days on Savoy Hill when Stewart Hibberd had announced me and I gave topical travel talks. But this was a tougher assignment altogether and I took it seriously, and would have been what was called by the men about me a prick, if I had not done so.

In an old box of odd notes and MSS from wartime I have found the script of that broadcast, as I wrote it with my rum ration beside me in the POs' Mess. Dog-eared and discoloured, it is covered with the scrawly handwriting of the time and I should like dearly to sub-edit it now and cut out a few of its ineptitudes. But I leave it exactly as it is. It will demonstrate at least the preoccupations of 1942.

I expect most of you had lectures on Security while we were still in Scotland, and I daresay some of you are pretty browned off with the whole subject. But it has suddenly become vitally important. I really don't think it would be any exaggeration to say that in this operation Security is as important as air supremacy, command of the sea, communications, or any other of the factors of war we hear so much about. I believe that whether or not the troops of this convoy manage to keep their mouths shut in Durban will be as decisive a factor as the way in which they actually fight when we reach the objective.

Why? Because, without any question at all, in Durban are a number of ladies and gentlemen impatiently awaiting our arrival. They won't come down to the docks to meet us, they won't wave any flags or call attention to themselves. If you want to be polite to these ladies and gentlemen you will call them 'enemy agents', but I prefer the old-fashioned blunt word '*spies*'.

It sounds a little melodramatic, I know. Like a Garbo picture or a novel by William le Queux. In England we're apt to think of spies as almost imaginary characters. We've heard of them as we've heard of ghosts or fairies, but because we've never to our knowledge seen them, we think of them as something unreal. That's the very greatest mistake we can possibly make. They are only too real. Their existence, and their existence in Durban, is as certain as our own.

What will they be like? If I could tell you that, if I could teach you, in ten easy lessons, how to recognize an enemy spy, it would all be too easy. Perhaps you think of the spy as a luscious blonde with the plans of the fort stuffed between her bristols. Or as the mysterious bearded stranger with the dark glasses who sits in the corner of a railway carriage busily taking down soldiers' talk in shorthand. Those are the novelist's idea. Whatever else the spy is, he or she will be essentially ordinary, probably very pleasant, certainly not at all foreign, or mysterious. He may be in uniform. He may be a barman. He may be a cheerful hospitable bloke you meet in a pub.

But the danger to us is not in any direct contact with him. He is no fool. He has probably never spoken to a British soldier. Why should he need to? All he has to do is to meet, and talk to, and listen to, his friends and acquaintances who have met the troops. He may be a bank clerk or a shop assistant who doesn't even go out much in the evening. If soldiers talk, if *we* talk, to *anyone*, sooner or later he will know what we said. So we don't even need to be suspicious of strangers we meet. They may be completely innocent. They may ask us questions out of mere personal interest or curiosity. And still the information we give them will find its way sooner or later to the interested parties.

Now what information do they chiefly want from us? First and foremost they want the information that we want ourselves—where we're going. Well, we don't know. It may be that no one on this ship knows, yet. But we've all got our guesses. And its these guesses that the enemy agent would like to hear. If he hears, even, that we don't suppose we're bound for Egypt or Burma, but for some special job, the information is of real value to him, and to the German and Japanese High Commands. Secondly, he wants to know who we are, what units are in the convoy. That would be real meat for him. He might get an Iron Cross from the Fuehrer for finding that out. And that makes it hardest of all for us—we've not got even to reveal our own regiments. I know that's hard. If you're having a drink with a South African soldier or civilian and he asks what you're in, you feel a bit of a twirp if you can't tell him. But you've got to get out of it somehow. Somewhere in Berlin is a neat file-index in which are all the details of your battalion, its personnel, its experience, the name of its commanding officer, the kind of training it has had. If Jerry knows you're in this convoy he can form a pretty good idea of what this convoy is for. He *mustn't* know you're in this convoy.

Then he'll want to know a great number of other facts —our escort through the bay, the ships at Freetown, what tanks and planes we have with us, where we were stationed in Great Britain, our equipment, our strength. I'm not suggesting that any of you are such fools as to discuss these things with strangers, but it is only too easy to mention some trivial fact which gives away information about them when you least expect it. And it isn't only strangers. Some of you have friends, even relatives, in Durban whom you know are 100% with us. Even to them you mustn't talk indiscreetly. They aren't agents, but they may unwittingly pass on information. There's a good old Arab proverb—'Thy friend has a friend, and thy friend's friend a friend. Beware.'

There's another thing. The MO has already given us his advice about women. As a doctor he is chiefly concerned with them as carriers of VD. As a Security man I'm chiefly concerned with them as carriers of information. Ever since warfare has existed whores have been used to obtain information from soldiers. They're ideal for the purpose. They can ask questions without arousing suspicion, and they've no scruples about selling their information. So if you do ignore the doctor's advice, for God's sake do your stuff without nattering. It should be easy enough. If you go to bed with a woman remember— there may be a Jerry under *your* bed.

I want to say a little about letters and cables and things.

I know that there is an idea in the Army that its rather clever to beat the censorship. Perhaps you have thought that when you get ashore you'll be able to write and post a letter back to England, and no one will be any the wiser. Well, I don't think that would be very smart really. In the first place all mail leaving South Africa for home is censored. If you put your name on the letter it will be traced to you, and you face a court-martial charge. If you don't put your name and address on it, it simply doesn't leave Durban. The same applies to cables. But its not because you are certain to be caught if you try to beat the censorship that I stress the matter, but because it is, after all, a rather cheap and mean thing to do. We're all in this outfit together, and between us we've got to make it a success or a balls-up. A balls-up means big casualties, besides making any of us who survive look fools in the eyes of the world. And there's no surer way of making it a balls-up than advertising through written messages or letters which may fall into anyone's hands, just where we are and what we're doing.

I know that all this isn't easy. You may be quite determined now not to spill the beans when you get ashore. You think there've been enough beans on this ship already. But it's going to be harder than you think. A couple of pints after a month without beer, and most of us will be ready to talk our heads off. And somehow or other I want to try and get you to see what madness that will be. We know for certain that Enemy Intelligence is not only very active in South Africa, but that it has excellent means of communication. Even since we've been on this ship, as you may have heard on the S. African news, three more German agents have been charged there with communicating details of British convoys bound for the East. And this is no ordinary convoy. Enemy Intelligence is going to strain every nerve to find out about this. And we've got to beat it. The temptation will be for a man to bum his load about this job. When he meets a South African who tells him his brother was at Tobruk and cousin took Addis Abbaba, he'll be apt to say—yes, that's all very well, but this thing *we're* on . . . and so on. It's dead easy. Because after all, this operation is the goods. But its a temptation we've got to resist.

And don't think I'm asking you all this for the sake of authority. I'm not asking you to keep your mouths shut because your officers, or the War Office, or the Government, or any big cheese, orders it. I'm asking it for our own sakes, yours and mine, and for the sake of every one in the convoy. One bloody fool with the wrong patter can sink the whole shooting match. This is not an appeal to you to be good, and obey orders. I've no more respect for orders than you have. But it is an appeal, and a very urgent appeal, to think of your own skin—and those of your friends. I don't want to be chewed by sharks in the Indian Ocean or knackered by Japanese gunmen. So once again I ask you —for God's sake remember ashore, and all the time ashore, whoever you're with and whatever you're doing, wherever you go or however you're treated, don't talk about anything military at all. It should be a relief to forget you're soldiers for a while. Tell the women how delightful they are and the men what a grand place Durban is. But forget the names of your regiment, your ship, your officers, forget what kind of training you've had and what equipment you've got, forget what kind of a job you think it is and what kind of troops you are. Then we may have a chance to beat the rooting swine at their own game, and get to our objective unmolested, and spring a real surprise on the enemy. It depends on you. That's not bullshit. It absolutely depends on you.

CHAPTER NINE

Durban

[1]

A GOOD many thousand men of the British forces during the last war must have shared the experience, touched with paradisal fantasy, of arriving in a port of South Africa and being whisked away by hospitable people unknown to them previously to be given what seemed to them, after years of home shortages and Service life, something like their hearts' desire. It was altogether too lavish for belief, the welcome we received in Durban in late April 1942, though many convoys had passed through before us and, one would have supposed, tried the tolerance and open-handedness of their hosts.

For me, for many years, South Africa had a particular, somewhat romantic appeal perhaps because my mother's youngest brother, my Uncle Toby, Stanley Shelbourne Taylor who was a KC. at the South African Bar, had been a heroic figure in my childhood, but more probably because an old writer named Douglas Blackburn had enlivened my years at Tonbridge by telling me stories of elephants' dying grounds, Illicit Diamond Buying and gun-running. He had been a journalist on the Johannesburg *Star* and founded the *Sentinel* which he published in Krugersdorp; had been, as it seemed to me, everywhere and done everything, before, during and after the South African War, and he gave me copies of his books *Prinsloo of Prinsloodorp*, a *Burgher Quixote* and the rest which I have to this day. I described him in a book in this sequence, *The Altar in the Loft*.

I am not suggesting that I remembered either of these two men as I went down the gangplank in Durban. But I was prepared for wonders. I was alone and gloating over this opportunity to enter an unvisited continent. South Africa had seemed immensely remote in those days before air travel made it accessible to anyone with money enough to pay the fare, and it was still less than fifty years since Rider Haggard had published *King Solomon's Mines* and sixty since the Zulu War. I doubt if anyone else in that convoy thought of this visit to Durban as a bonus of experience notched up on the credit side in a writer's account book.

For that first evening ashore I resolved to remain alone. I passed the cars lining the docks, owned by the kindly people of Durban seeking whom they might entertain, and followed a street towards the centre, which was not brightly lit, though the fruit in a lighted shop was, or seems in retrospect, like a heap of brilliant crystals and I stopped to buy a pound of grapes and walked on eating them, leaving a trail of skins and pips. The fruit was so improbable there in the dim street—we had not seen a banana or an orange for years. It remained irresistible to our troops throughout our stay and you would pass a soldier returning to his ship laden with fruit like a picture of Plenty with her cornucopia, grapes dropping from a paper bag, pineapples thrusting their leaves from his trouser pockets, mangoes or a bunch of lichees in his hands, oranges in the pockets of his shirt as though he had a woman's breasts.

I had purchased a pair of drill slacks from a RSF sergeant and had civilian shoes and wore these comfortably, but most soldiers were forced to go ashore in the ridiculous tropical kit of the time, indeterminate trousers made to turn down as 'long' or roll up as 'short' and serving as neither, with hot woollen half-stockings and an old-fashioned topee like a woman's gardening bonnet. Their knees and necks showed white and their faces streamed with sweat while the South Africans they met looked cool and well-groomed.

[2]

It was the lights of Durban which most dazzlingly shine out

in my memory of that first night ashore, the lights in the broad white streets which gave the city an other-worldly aspect after the blacked-out sombreness of England. The Zulu rickshaw boys in their many-coloured finery were deliberately grotesque, their feathers and beads a disguise more than a touch of natural colour. I took them for granted, I think, something to be expected in South Africa but I must have gaped at the lights and the fruit and the shop-windows piled high with things I had not seen on sale in England in 'living memory'—that was for the last two years.

The men of the convoy enjoyed natural excesses of liberation from their troop-decks, excesses which lasted for all the days they remained ashore and were accepted by the people of Durban with an astonishing good grace. They would harass but enrich the rickshaw boys, overcrowd the bars, fight on the pavements, make wild, unnecessary purchases, stream through the streets in linked cordons singing uproariously, bribe taxi-drivers to take them to shebeens, or, seized with nostalgic emotionalism, seek out mission-houses and religious canteens to shout the more waltz-like and sentimental hymn-tunes till there were tears in their own eyes and those of the lady helpers who heard them.

There would be pitched battles at street-corners between men of two units, or between services, fights which would end in the arrival of the Military Police van, a few arrests, a deal of loquacious handshaking and a search for the nearest bar where eternal amity between the combatants would be pledged in lager beer. In public gardens you would come on khaki-clad figures stretched out under the trees in stertorous sleep; on every public seat in the city were men and girls huddled and compressed, oblivious of all but one another's feverish flesh. The dance halls and cinemas were crowded beyond natural endurance, and little shops selling shoddy souvenirs would remain open till the small hours. Restaurants of every kind were plentiful and cheap, but the most prosperous were those fish and chip saloons which most resembled their counterparts in

Hull or Holloway, though the city was cosmopolitan enough if one looked for foreignness.

The next day there was one of those exhibitions of naivety from the Ib staff which filled me with cynicism then and thereafter. We were called together by some GSO, an ex-schoolmaster who had received a commission shortly before.

"As FS men," he said, "I want you to undertake certain duties while we're in port here. We want to give the impression that our part of the convoy is bound for North Africa."

"Where *is* it bound for?" asked someone curtly.

The GSO (1, 2 or 3, I forget now) became rather coy.

"Ah. That would be telling wouldn't it? The important thing is that you should spread the information that we're going North, like other convoys."

"We were taught at Matlock," I said because I was mischievous enough to want to rile him, "that it was dangerous to spread false information as cover for the truth. It often tells more than silence."

The GSO gave a superior smile.

"That was Matlock," he said. "You can forget most of that now. This is the real thing."

"You'd scarcely think so," I said, seeing an argument was inevitable. "When you tell a dozen men to spread a story in a city of a quarter of a million people. How will we go about it?"

"I leave that to your ingenuity, if you have any. There are several obvious places in which to talk. Pubs, I suppose, canteens, barbers' shops. Particularly barbers' shops. Great places for gossip, those."

"How many times should we have our hair cut?"

"Don't be fatuous, Croft-Cooke. Just drop a seed of information here or there."

The notion was so far-fetched that I abandoned that aspect of it for things of more moment.

"What about expenses?" I asked. I knew there was a certain amount, probably very little, allotted to Ib, chiefly for officers.

"Expenses?" shouted the GSO. "What expenses?"

"Well, haircutting, for one. We can't go into barbers' shops without spending money, can we? Or pubs. Or canteens."

"Wouldn't you go to them in any case?"

"Not canteens," I said. "And only one barber's shop."

"I see you've entirely failed to get the idea. Any other questions?"

Nobody had any other questions and as the GSO seemed rather short of answers, this was as well.

That night I decided to go out on the town with an RSF sergeant who promised me he'd 'paint the whole fook'n place red'.

"I'll show you," Jock said. "How to have a good time in this fook'n town. I've been here before."

It would have been a less eventful, but also a less memorable evening if I had not betrayed the highest principles of textbook Security by telling Jock of the ridiculous instructions of the GSO.

"I'll drop a fook'n seed of information here and there," said Jock. He was a short, study fellow, incurably argumentative and energetic, and he had, like all of us, drawn his back pay for the weeks he had been at sea.

We started inevitably in a bar.

"Do you know what they drink in this fook'n town, Max? Fook'n brandy and ginger ale! It's piss but it gives results. Let's try it."

We did, with some effect, and half an hour later Jock was ready for 'any fook'n thing'. (Hereafter I will take most of his qualifying adjectives as read.) We called a rickshaw drawn by an enormous negro with an ostrich-feather head-dress.

"Take us to a barber's shop," said Jock making cut-throat gestures which interested but did not scare the Zulu. "Banana-walla," he further explained, for all overseas languages were alike to Jock. "Malum? Tick hai!"

The barber was alone and about to close. I think he was a Greek. Jock entered the shop and possessed himself of a razor. The barber, who thought it was a hold-up, became scared and the rickshaw boy who remained outside watched impassively with open jaw.

"Listen to me, you blathering little greaser," Jock said. "D'ye know where we're going?"

The barber shook his head.

"We're going to fook'n Iceland, see? You tell every one of your customers when they ask you. You say we're going to Iceland. Will you mind that? Iceland."

The barber nodded.

"Tell all the spies and fifth columnists I told you. And don't you fook'n forget it or I'll come back and murder you."

The barber, whose eyes had never left Jock since we entered, looked relieved as we moved to leave.

"How was that, Max?" Jock asked. "I told you I'd drop a few seeds. Let's find another pub because the bastards close early if we don't watch it."

Jock's next urge was to have a fight with someone, fortunately not myself, and he achieved it after two more brandy and ginger-ales. There was no malice in this—it was a necessary part of a good evening and almost anyone would serve as an antagonist. In fact it was a hefty lance-corporal of the CMP trying persuasively, with two others, to close the bar. I was warned of what would happen by Jock's quick aside to me—"See you later."

He did not start one of those long hostile arguments which are beloved of Glaswegians, but suddenly butted the lance-jack with a ferocious jerk of his head to the other's chin. Then with the agility of a wild animal he dived through the crowd and was gone before the CMP reached the door. There was no sign of him in the street and I thought he was lost for the night, but ten minutes later he signalled me from the door of a taxi he had booked, driven by a European or Anglo-Indian who kept asking nervously where we wanted to go.

"The hell out of here," said Jock. "Find some women. Savvy? Women. Knocking-shop. Get going."

The taximan drove out to a quiet suburb inhabited by

respectable Indians, told Jock that in the little balconied villa surrounded by bougainvillea bushes he would find what he wanted, turned quickly in the road and disappeared by the way we had come.

"Come on, Max," Jock said impatiently and knocked at the front door.

Whether that quiet suburban house really was a brothel, or whether the taxi-driver was working off some spite or vengeance of his own, I never discovered because the door remained closed.

"Let's break the bastard door down," said Jock. "The place is full of women. I can smell them."

He picked up a huge stone from the road and started to hammer furiously. This roused the district and I remember a little group, an old man armed with a long pole and several orientals of non-combatant appearance who came to protect their property. Although the night was full of noise no police appeared.

After that my recollections become vaguer. Jock demanded a shebeen.

"We'll get some of their own liquor if we can't get anything else," he said. I remember drinking something very raw and nasty, watched by unfriendly spectators, and I remember being on the long wooden balcony of a house with non-Europeans coming and going, examining us and prescribing hot coffee, which Jock said would make him sick.

"And listen, you!" he said aggressively. "We're going to fook'n Iceland. Mind that. Tell all the customers in this knocking-shop that we're going to Iceland."

Which may not have been what the GSO intended by 'dropping a few seeds' but was probably just as effective as carrying out his instructions.

[3]

The next evening after suffering from a hang-over all day

I joined Maurice Ohana for a quiet dinner in a good restaurant he had discovered. Maurice had been on the *Winchester Castle,* another ship in our convoy with Annis and the rest of the Section. They were to join us from here onwards. Maurice had enjoyed the voyage out, for there was a good piano on the ship and he had managed to get some work done.

We walked up from the docks together. Even in those days a natural cosmopolitan, Maurice found Durban, which had for him none of the magic it had for me as a gateway to a mysterious and exciting South Africa, a brash and rather provincial city, but he meant, as we all did, to enjoy it. The restaurant he had found *was* good and the wine—in retrospect, anyway—was superb. It was over that meal that Maurice made a remark which I have remembered ever since. "If only the French had colonized this country instead of the English and Dutch!" he sighed, thinking of the gorgeous raw materials in food which it possessed, like the steak we were eating then. I saw exactly what he meant.

But on the following morning something happened which changed the whole complexion of that first stay in Durban and give it a particular delight. I discovered that a man whom I had not seen for many years, who had been one of the major influences in my boyhood and afterwards, was here in the city, working at the Broadcasting Station. I have told his story in two earlier books* and will describe here only what it meant to me to find him and learn a great deal about the country from him. It happened like this.

I was in a place which I remember was not exactly like a continental café, though it had tables at which men drank beer and talked during the morning—rather like a Buenos Aires café in the Calle Florida. A man approached me, middle-aged, serious, and evidently kindly disposed. His object was a curious one. He had it in his head that every British soldier who came to South Africa had some connection, some relative or acquaintance, in the country whom he would like to dis-

* *The Drums of Morning* (1961) and *The Numbers Came* (1962).

cover. He had apparently been successful in putting men in touch with childhood friends, scarcely known kinsmen and for all I know absconding wives. He asked me if I knew anyone here. No, I said. Surely *someone*? Most Durban people were of British origin. Couldn't I remember someone who had once gone out to South Africa and never returned?

I thought of my uncle who had retired from the Bar and become a director of some Oppenheimer concern in London. I thought of Douglas Blackburn, dead these fourteen years, and again shook my head. The poor man seemed disappointed and I thought again. Then I remembered Oswald Horrax who had come out here to teach and of whom I had heard nothing for more than a decade. I tried the name and the effect was electrifying.

"Horrax?" said my well-meaning acquaintance. "Did you say Oswald Horrax? Spelt with ax?" He was so excited that he could scarcely bring out his news. "He's . . . I can put you in touch with him in a moment. Not five minutes from here. The broadcasting station. He's our best . . . Wait, I'll telephone. He's a broadcaster."

So within half an hour I was with Oswald. It was soon evident that one great good fortune at least had come to him. He had found a calling which used his varied talents. He was on the staff of the Durban broadcasting station, and an intelligent director, younger than Oswald, had given him his head. He was compère, disc jockey, critic, producer and actor. He gave talks and did a cross-talk act which had enormous local popularity. For all I know he was Uncle Oswald of Children's Hour and the emergency pianist. He was busy and at home, his youthful enthusiasm bursting through an authoritative manner. In his appearance there was only one change and it was for the better. His short thick unruly hair had turned white, not the dull grey of northern peoples but that bright silvery white which seems peculiar to Americans and South Africans.

Sitting in his airy flat that evening I came under the spell of his enthusiastic personality as I had in walks to the Wrekin a quarter of a century earlier. Then he had fired me with curiosity to read the novels of Conrad, Hardy, Hewlett or the poetry of the Catholic poets Belloc, Chesterton, Francis Thompson and Alice Meynell. Now it was of Africa that he discoursed, or rather of Africans, for he was truly interested in them and Africans to him were the Bantu peoples, particularly the Zulus. He had taught in an up-country mission school and learned a great deal about the race among whom he lived. His flat was full of small objects of native handicraft and he showed me photographs of his journeys in Bechuanaland. He 'opened vistas' as the saying is, and even as a soldier, bound for an unknown destination, part of an organized and disciplined force, I was carried away by the idea of Africa, of learning about it and eventually writing about it. It seemed to me, that evening in Oswald's flat, the one subject I wanted to write about, the one exploration I wanted to make. I knew nothing of the Zulus then, except their name and a few facts of their history. I would learn, I decided, forgetting the mission on which I was bound and the military bonds which tied me.

"I tell you what," said Oswald. "There is a Zulu dancing competition tomorrow. Several hundred dancers in vast co-ordinated groups. It's well worth watching. Would you like to come?"

Would I? So I saw one of the most remarkable exhibitions of mass dancing in the modern world. Exhibition? No, Ngoma dancing was not an exhibition. The dancers were too self-absorbed, too indifferent to everything but their own impulses to provide what could be called an exhibition, though it took place in a public park and was watched by spectators who were outnumbered by the dancers themselves. It was breathtaking. Teams of fifty to seventy men lined up one after another, the riotous colour of their dress and accoutrements flashing and their ebony skins glistening against the green background of the park's lawns; they might have been preparing for a savage war against others of their race, though this was not a war dance. They pounded the earth with the soles of their feet in resounding unison, as though they were trying to drive their naked feet into the ground. They danced as though every gesture was the most vigorous that could be made, as though they were willing their bodies to undertake yet wilder tasks of strength. They showed, not hostility to an enemy but the unselfconscious dynamism of wild animals.

Each group had a leader and moved rhythmically to his command, but the rhythm was not that of music, delicate and restrained, rather the rhythm of the sea or of thunder. They were fighting, not with an enemy, but with themselves, as though they wanted yet more impossible achievements, to fly, to swim over the earth, to make themselves into swords or arrows, or into lions or deer. I cannot remember what music, if any, was heard. I suppose there were drums, though they seem scarcely to have been necessary, such was the human drumbeat of the dance.

When I look over the printed programme of that afternoon's 'Native Dancing Championships' it seems oddly dated. Messages from the Secretary for Native Affairs and lists of prizes from which one learns that 'every dancer taking part will be presented with a Badge of recognition', and a note that 'it is very gratifying to find so many of Durban's citizens who are employers of native labour supporting this excellent endeavour to provide better facilities for native recreation. As Chairman of the Native Administration Committee I feel sure that the native population of Durban will be most grateful for the interest taken on their behalf, and I have no doubt those who have the privilege of seeing those dances will appreciate the skill and enthusiasm shown by the dancers.'

Is there still Ngoma dancing in the park in Durban? Do three score Zulus in unison thump the ground with the soles of their feet to produce one earth-shaking thud, while spectators of British origin whose forebears had fought against them in the Zulu Wars watch appreciatively? I fear that even an interest in that fantastic spectacle would be accounted now dangerously misplaced or at the least sentimental and eccentric.

This was, after all, in the era of Smuts, a sane and cheerful time for South Africans of all races, which will not return.

[4]

For the rest of that stay in Durban I spent most of the time with Oswald and his wife and the young director of broadcasting. I broadcast twice at a guinea or two a time—a useful increment—but forget what I talked about. Our own Security regulations made it necessary for permission to be obtained for my broadcasts from the officer commanding the whole operation, Lieutenant-General R. G. Sturges, and on the day on which I was due to go on the air young Annis set out to obtain that permission, only to find that the General was asleep. It seemed immensely important to me to earn my guineas and I persuaded Annis to persist. The General awoke an hour before the broadcast and said simply "Why not?"

Two days later we sailed for Madagascar.

Here the narrative breaks, because my story of the campaign and the six months I spent on the island has already been recounted in *The Blood-Red Island* (1953). But between our occupation of the northern tip of Madagascar and our landings at Majuunga and Tamatave we were taken for some reason to Mombasa and that extraordinary city seems worth recalling before I return to Natal for the remainder of my time there.

[5]

When I remember my short stay in Mombasa and what I did there, I think I must have been touched by the African sun. For in the middle of two campaigns in Madagascar, about to take part in further landings there, living under canvas in a transit camp outside Mombasa itself and knowing that it could not be for more than a week or two, I began to 'settle in', to 'learn about the place', even in a sense to 'get my feet under the table' (as the Royal Marines used to say when they were given hospitality), all as if I should remain here till the end of the war, or longer. I started to learn the language—Arabic, not Swahili —and have a notebook of two hundred pencilled words to prove it, from *ana*, I, to *hebbuk*, love, all written down with great care. I made friends and formed habits, I explored every quarter of the town and would soon have become a familiar figure in at least three of them if we had not received orders to embark again.

My excuse is that Mombasa seemed to me an intensely interesting place. Its history was full of fighting between Portuguese and Arabs, a history as violent and colourful as that of Zanzibar. There were monuments and temples of all the gods, and winding streets through the various quarters, Arab, Indian and old Jewish. The tarmac European—or, as one dared say then, British quarter—was of moment only as providing good restaurants where curry in great variety was served by Swahili waiters in a somewhat wardroom atmosphere. I have read somewhere 'the climate of Mombasa is not unhealthful and Europeans live there in tolerable comfort'. You bet they bloody do, I thought at the time, cramped from the troopdecks of a hell ship called ironically *The Empire Pride*. But I ate well in the European restaurants of Mombasa and went from them to the winding lanes among fine old houses which I came to delight in.

There was a clean, fairly wide cobbled street which ran through the old Jewish quarter where there were carved doorways and an atmosphere clear of traffic and dust. But more attractive to me were the narrow and windowless streets of the Arab town. Here I took up my quarters for the stay—not sleeping quarters, for I went nightly on my motor bike to the transit camp, but idling quarters, talking quarters, coffee-drinking quarters, in a tiny shop selling groceries, with whose proprietor I could only communicate by signs and smiles. What first took me there I do not remember but the Arab, who wore a turban, I seem to recall, and sometimes had his children about him, put a chair out for me and on this I sat day by day till the hot-coffee salesman with his great brass urn and tinkling metal cups came down the street and offered us coffee to which a pinch of ginger was added. It was my first brief experience of the Arab world and was not to be renewed till I came to Tangier in 1954.

I daresay that city, almost free from traffic except in the European centre, would be unrecognizable today. Giant office and apartment blocks have probably been built and what was the quiet old Jewish quarter is now a residential area, and I would no longer be tempted to think, as I did then, how pleasant it would be to own one of those ancient houses with the carved doorways and learn to speak Arabic so that I could do more than merely smile and gesture to my friends.

CHAPTER TEN

Mtubatuba

[1]

In Madagascar I had a severe attack of malaria and after we had left the island and been brought back to South Africa it came again. I was with my Section in a transit camp in Pietermaritzburg waiting to embark for India, when the fever struck and I was ordered to hospital. This seemed a calamity at the time but like so many calamities in the Army it turned out to be a boon. For the fortnight I spent in a Pietermaritzburg hospital separated me from the rest of my Section who went on to Bombay and hung about there for three months while I was left behind on my own. I belonged to no unit and was able to lead an entirely civilian life in Durban, to visit areas of Zululand on leave, to earn a living above my sergeant's pay, which of course continued, by broadcasting and journalism, and do what I had wanted to do on the first visit, learn what I could of South Africa and its peoples.

Discharged from hospital I came down to Durban through the Valley of a Thousand Hills and reported to Clarewood Camp, in which most of the remainder of the Combined Ops Force was stationed, the RSFs, the Gunners and the RTR with whom I had travelled out from England, and men of other units in the 29th Independent Brigade known to me only by sight, with all of whom I had been in Madagascar.

I found the Brigade Major, John Ridell, who was a deep-voiced man with a large moustache (the brother-in-law of Brigadier Festing*), in a tent somewhere among the miles of

* Later Field Marshal Sir Francis Festing, GCB, KBE, DSO.

146

tents in that huge encampment, and asked for instructions. He gave them briefly, and as I soon realized, fatefully.

"You'd better go away on leave and come back when you want some money," were his exact words, which became, as they say, printed on my heart. I followed them exactly for three months.

I had money, some thirty or forty pounds stitched in a body belt. By the standards of that time and place I was rich, and would be given a railway warrant for anywhere I chose to go on leave. I had no responsibilities or obligations and as a British soldier in South Africa I was incredibly privileged and spoilt by the inhabitants. Perhaps never, before or since, have I felt so free and so thrilled by the sense of a new world about me, which waited to be explored.

I decided to see something of Zululand and asked the advice of Oswald Horrax, who not realizing quite what I had in mind, suggested that I should go up the coast to St Lucia Bay, in which he had once spent a pleasant holiday. This meant a long train journey and at every station there were crowds of Bantu workers loading sugar cane with treacly hands, looking soiled and wretchedly dressed in a kind of sackcloth. I found St Lucia Bay occupied by the RAF and turned inland to a place named Mtubatuba which promised to be more typical of the country.

From there I made, quite unimpeded, a number of incursions into Zulu areas. I suppose that on paper these were no more than observant journeys by car and bus, but for me they were a deliberate assault on the sanctuaries of the Zulu, an exploration to gain knowledge of another people, to see an unfamiliar landscape and learn the traditions and mythology of a race—at that time at least—almost untouched by European influence or custom. A people with a life of their own, visible to all the world but noted by few, whose naive secrets were immensely worth discovering.

The hotel at Mtubatuba was a white modern building in which good meals (of curry chiefly) were served and, I suspected, cooked by Indians. There were hearty English breakfasts enjoyed before the sun was fully up, and a bar in which the neighbouring farmers met, while all round the hotel was heard the faint sough and rattle of eucalyptus trees. The little town had no more than twenty or thirty European houses, but there were four stores in which the Zulus crowded. When one entered these they continued to seem lazy and remote though their eyes glittered watchfully. Half naked women with naked children slung on their backs fingered articles which they pondered dreamily, some of them wearing their hair caked with clay and red ochre. When they finally decided on a purchase from the Indians who kept the store, it was nearly always cloth, I noticed, and having come to the point of making their bargain they would carry their parcels away swiftly and secretively.

At the local police station, a stone building having behind it two rows of small thatched huts in each of which a Zulu policeman lived with or without his family, there was only one white officer, a Sergeant Archer who wore a service ribbon from the First World War, though he was younger than I and had to explain that he had not actually been in the Services but needed at least one ribbon for his job. He was a friendly and helpful man who assumed responsibility for my education in the ways of the people whom he, and every other European, called 'the natives'.

His Zulu policemen were issued with assegais and two of them dressed themselves in full regalia for a photograph, with leopard-skin head-dress and loin-cloths of undressed calf-skin. They posed delightedly with *ihwu*, shields, held high, and in their huts I saw for the first time one of the things that most impressed me about the Zulus, that every object of utility in their homes from beer-pots, *ukamba,* to trays, *uggoko,* was ornamented or carved, each a thing of beauty with nothing shoddy or foreign in the hut to spoil the effect of airy, fresh-smelling cleanliness and order. Men and women made me welcome, but here, as so often in South Africa, I came unexpectedly on disturbing evidence that under their smiles and seeming happiness there was often serious discontent.

One of the policemen spoke English. He was, Sergeant Archer told me with unconcealed disgust, mission-educated. Since the only newspaper which came—so far as I could see— to Mtubatuba was to be seen in his hut, I took to calling there for 'a read of the paper.' He offered this politely but he could not be drawn into any kind of discussion until one morning, just as I was leaving, he suddenly said quite distinctly "They treat us like dirt." Nothing more, and I do not profess to have seen in his eyes more than the usual black impassive stillness, or heard in his voice any half-suppressed fury. But he meant it, and he meant me to know it.

I began to notice other things about the people which seemed to me significant. The Zulu was never seen without some kind of stick, a heavy knob-kerry, *ewese*, which some might well consider a war-club, or a lighter one, *sakele,* which could still crack a skull like an egg, or a fighting-stick, *bokwe*, carved and pointed to poke out a man's eye, or a courting-stick bound with wire, *esketo*. Although on ceremonial occasions like his wedding-day he carried an umbrella or sunshade, he never seemed far from what we should consider arms. Moreover, though the organizers of that dance competition in Durban strongly denied that any of the dances were war dances, it is impossible to accept that only thirty years after the death of Dinizulu, and five more from the end of the last Zulu Rising, these had become a naturally pacific people. As I learned later, one of their most fierce resentments at that time was that they, the greatest warriors of southern Africa, had not been recruited to fight in the war of the white men overseas, except to act as stretcher-bearers and such. With a sense of the proper usages of war they had recovered a flag from an Italian ship sunk off the coast after it had escaped from Durban on Italy's declaration of war, and hung it in the police station instead of looting the wreck for lavatory-bowls, apparently her chief cargo.

Sergeant Archer invited me to accompany him on an expedition and we set out by car with the two policemen who had worn their regalia for a photograph, now dressed very differently, with burnished buttons and para-military uniforms. We drove towards a cattle-market and passed a herd of goats being taken to it by a small boy who sank into the grass on our approach and when told to stand up covered his eyes with his hand, averting the evil eye of the white men perhaps. The market was conducted by a European auctioneer, cattle being graded in lots of eight or ten.

At Hlabisa a Magistrate's Court was in session and I watched while three cases of native offences were dealt with by a white magistrate. A man who had been twice imprisoned and once deported to Portuguese East Africa was charged with dealing in illicit liquor. His defence was that the police had substituted the liquor for his harmless lemonade in order to frame him. Next came a man and woman 'taken in adultery'; they were fined and released. A Zulu schoolmaster was also fined for assaulting the police. From the court-house we went to a store kept by a couple of British origin, Mr and Mrs Irons, who gave us tea and home-made cakes in a cool rondavel open to the thatched roof above us.

Thence to the Hluhluwe Game Reserve where the southern white rhinoceros had its last home. We drove for about a mile towards the headquarters of the game warden, Captain Potter, without seeing anything more startling than antelopes, but the drive had an eerie fascination about it which came from the very name of Reserve. One expected large pachyderms to shoulder their way between the trees and block our road. Captain Potter promised me a zebra skin, an object I had long wanted to acquire because there is no more attractive form of floor covering. But the promise was never fulfilled.

It was a mile or two after we had left the game reserve that we came on a giant monitor lizard, sunning itself on a bank beside the road. Sometimes miscalled iguana, the monitor is a large and harmless creature but from its size alone it has the frightening aspect of some prehistoric monster. The two policemen ran to capture it but it quickly disappeared in an ant-bear's hole and had to be dug out hissing with menace but unable to defend itself. The two Zulus showed no fear of it, but when I picked up its body, all six feet of it, one of them leaped aside thinking I was going to throw it at him. "Why did they kill it?" I asked, feeling some compunction. "Good to eat," Archer explained, and I find that according to *Larousse Gastronomique* the iguana is considered a gourmet's delicacy.

[2]

On another occasion I went with Sergeant Archer to call on Chief Mtubatuba himself. This almost legendary figure whose forebears had given their name to the whole district, though his own surname was Mkwanazi, was said to be nearly ninety years old and to have over a thousand living descendants. He owned a hundred thousand head of cattle and was known to be worth over a million pounds, but was extortionate with his own people, fining them an ox or two for any tribal offence reported to him. His kraals, scattered about the countryside, numbered over a dozen and in each he kept six or eight wives and a number of dependants and relatives.

His dealings were all in cash; when he went to the cattle market he was accompanied by his young men, one of whom carried a suitcase of pound notes. He had recently purchased a new motor car for £800, paying £600 of it with silver coins.

He kept up a state of dignity and ceremony, but it would not be recognized as that by anyone unaccustomed to the ways of his people. The kraal to which we went was not large, perhaps a dozen huts round that of Mtubatuba himself, and as we approached there were not more than a score of people, wives and dependants, in sight. The old man kept us waiting for the five minutes or so prescribed by protocol and when we were admitted to his hut, we sat on a rawhide mat to the left of the entry, leaving two places for us between himself and the door. He looked ancient but tough and sinewy; I imagine his age had been exaggerated by report. One can calculate the age of the older Zulus by the year of their conscription to the impis, armies which fought the foreigners. Chief Mtubatuba was of the Falaza (Clouds of Heaven) conscription which suggests he was in his eighties at this time. Archer told me he drove down to the town once a month to be given an injection which enabled him to enjoy his wives.

The Chief wore a check-patterned blanket pulled round his shoulders, but artfully disposed here and in the photograph I took of him outside his hut to expose the *three* hefty gold watches he wore on his left wrist.

He asked Archer in Zulu who I was. A brother from across the sea, Archer said. From what place across the sea? England. How did I come here? With the English soldiers. This was fully digested, after which the Chief said I was welcome, and he was glad to see me.

He then turned, or so Archer told me afterwards, to discuss his health and Archer's, cattle prices and so on before mentioning that he had sent to summon the surviving son of one of his tribe who had died owing the State £9.

I looked about me as they talked, at the round hut painted on posts to a height of four feet and at the shrewd watchful old face of the Chief who, while he talked, never let go of a beaded purse. He had long well-kept finger-nails. He asked me to take a photograph of him, but he wanted to be seen alone, or alone with me, not among his people. When this was done I could take photographs of his wives of whom about a dozen had collected, including one magnificent tall bare-breasted creature with clipped hair and an insolent smile who shoved her way to the front of every group.

When we were about to leave, a magnificent ram was produced as the gift due to be presented by the Chief to his visitors. It was at once tethered in the back of our truck by Archer's two policemen and we drove away.

[3]

I went by bus to Nongoma, about forty miles away, and saw

the landscape grow more beautiful in the high veldt where, instead of scrub and low bushes, there were trees and bright green grass on the skyline against the brilliant blue of the African sky. I had been invited to the town by a very British couple named Jennings who had made a fine garden and collected African handicrafts. Their four-year-old son talked the difficult Zulu language.

Jennings told me that on the following day there was to be a prize-giving at the school at Mahasheni for children of the Royal House. Although I attended it, met the all-Bantu staff and many of the pupils, including Cyprian who was the chosen heir to the late King of the Zulus, and Godfrey the son of the Regent who appeared to be a probable rival for the throne, I have never been able to learn what has happened since then to those rival claimants, who were still in their 'teens. Information about the Zulu Royal Family does not leave the country or rouse much interest there.

The children were beautiful, the little girls of twelve, fully developed and ready for marriage, looking somewhat un-natural in the gym-dresses insisted on by the school, while the tall boys were no less out of place in their suits and ties and collars. There was a concert with songs by groups, 'the humming birds', 'the morning stars', 'the sweet roses' and 'the wild dogs', the feet and hands of the singers moving in rhythm. *Rule Britannia* was sung with a war-dance movement by the whole school. Afterwards was a PT display with a sort of barbaric parody of bull.

The royal home was half a mile away, a brick-built version of a kraal, the main house in the centre with a veranda and rondavels on each side. At every corner of the enclosure was a post ornamented with an antelope's head and horns, a pre-caution against lightning, 'just as you have lightning conductors' I was told.

After returning to Mtubatuba and saying goodbye to Archer and his policemen I went by train to Empangene where the hotel proprietress, whose name and perhaps birth were British, refused to give me my bill because her husand, she said, was a serving soldier. When I reached Stanger I found that I had left my body belt with all my money in my bedroom and had to wait for it to be sent on by registered post.

Stanger was then a town of Indians, descendants of those who had been introduced as labour for the sugar plantations but were now prosperous citizens who owned most of the houses in the town but had no say on the local council.

[4]

From Stanger I went to Mapamulo by a small bus driven by a young Afrikaans. I was asked to sit with the driver and a white-bearded French priest at the front of the bus and not among the Zulu women whose large brown breasts were exposed artlessly, or the men who stank of Zulu beer made of mealies, kaffir-corn and water.

The priest and I fell into conversation, shouting over the noise of the engine and rattle of the bodywork. His name was Father L'Hôte and he was in charge of a lonely mission in the hills beyond Mapamulo. It was called St Filomena's Catholic Mission and the priest had built it, church, school and mission-house, with concrete blocks which he had persuaded his first few converts to carry on their heads to the lonely site he had chosen. Now an old man, he had watched his Mission grow till it had a congregation of several hundred Zulus. During that lurching journey he invited me to stay with him at his mission-house and although I had to refuse since I was going to stay at Mapamulo with another kind of missionary, a Dr Hertslet, the Medical Officer in that isolated place, I went to the Mission later, as I shall recount. When we reached Mapamulo I enviously watched Father L'Hôte swing himself to the saddle of a horse kept waiting for him and ride away towards the hills.

Most small settlements in Zululand were very much alike at that time, a few European bungalows, a court house perhaps, a couple of Indian stores and sometimes a hotel to which the white farmers or government officials came, using it as a club.

But in Mapamulo Dr Hertslet and his wife were the only Europeans while he was the only Medical Officer for miles around. He was a tall, bearded man, a very hard worker and an able propagandist for the Zulu cause. He and his wife devoted their lives to the Zulus, loved them and lived among them, only coming down to Durban to arrange the publication of the books they wrote to defend the independence and promote the well-being of 'their people'. They had invited me, through Oswald Horrax, to stay with them and I did so gratefully.

Their home was simply furnished, surrounded with great trees and the kind of garden which people who love flowers but have no time to care for them more than occasionally, are apt to make. They knew the value of conversation in their own language which only came to them rarely with strangers, and at night we would sit on the veranda and talk for hours.

I was conscious there of that phenomenon, the vastness of the African night. I can only explain this, which will seem a meaningless cliché to many, with yet more clichés. Obviously hills are no farther away, the stars are not more remote in Africa than anywhere else, and the evening is not more silent. Yet there is a vastness about it which makes the Indian night close and intimate in comparison. I am not thinking of mountain scenery, or indeed scenery of any kind, but in Africa the moon and the stars seem unconcerned with us as we feel unconcerned with them. The religions of Asia and Europe for long saw the earth as the centre of a surrounding universe in which everything influenced or threatened mankind. For the African with his animism, his ancestor worship and witchcraft, the heavens did not descend or the stars indicate the future.

I learned a great deal from the Hertslets but it was, I recognize rather sadly, mostly textbook knowledge that could be gained from a good work of reference. They were not writers—except of propaganda—and could not communicate the odd and wonderful things, pregnant with situation and colour, which at that time I believed I wanted to know. They were working for the well-being of the Zulu, not watching his behaviour or discovering his character except in so far as a knowledge of these aided them in their work. But they seemed to recognize this themselves for with true generosity they introduced me to members of a Zulu family from whom I should learn what I wanted.

Caleb Gumede was a schoolmaster of twenty-seven who wore European clothes with evident distaste, a Tyrolean hat— heaven knows how come by—shirt, shorts, tattered stockings and uncomfortable shoes which he liked to kick off. He took me for a long trek across the hills to the kraal of a chief where I was welcomed and given my first draught of Zulu beer. I swallowed it manfully under the eyes of the Chief, Samuel Ntuli, who had once been a Christian minister but had returned to the land, bringing to his kraal a few pieces of town-made furniture. I realized here that although the entrance of the round hut alone gave it light, there was coolness under its thatched wooden framework, and as I became accustomed to the dim interior it seemed to grow lighter, till I could distinguish the faces of the men about me, some of whom wore tattered European clothes. Samuel Ntuli asked me, as every Zulu did, about the progress of the war and complained that his people could have no part in it. There were references to Queen Victoria and to British generals and governors whose names were still remembered. The huge beer pot seemed to remain beside me with a carved wood mug from which I drank. Had I had enough? Ntuli asked, as he wanted to hand the pot to others but could not do it, Caleb Gumede explained to me, until I as a visitor was satisfied. Each guest in turn was called up by the Chief and given his portion.

Later came an *amahubo,* a performance of dance and song combined. The singing started almost *sotto voce* with the chant of one old man, and was gradually taken up by all. The dancing too began with small gestures but grew—literally by leaps and bounds—until the dancers, among them one splendid youth, abandoned themselves wildly to the dance.

Caleb Gumede made nothing of the walk home, in spite of

his unaccustomed shoes, but I found the trek by footpaths between kraals and over hillsides fairly exhausting since it meant a total of some twenty-four miles covered since morning.

I had, after all, just recovered from a second bout of malaria. I was thin as a rake and though my driving curiosity about the places and people around me did not allow fatigue, I must have been in sorry condition. Hertslet insisted on examining me that evening and I still have the certificate he wrote out for me of which, needless to say, I never made use since it might have deprived me of the supreme experience to come, my three years in India.

Mapamulo
18 XII 42.

I have today Examined Staff Sergeant R. Croft-Cooke, who has been on leave in my district.

His blood-pressure is low 100/88, and his pulse is rapid 90–100.

I am of the opinion that he is *not* fit for the strains of Active Service.

The symptoms elicited confirm this opinion.

Lewis E. Hertslet
MRCS. RCP.
D.S.

[5]

Next day I met one of the most interesting men in my experience, Caleb Gumede's uncle Amos Hlalehlathi Gumede. Whether or not he could be called *izinyanga* or witch-doctor I cannot say. He was certainly a fortune-teller and the poet of many songs of praise known to his people. He was also a man of great dignity and courtesy whose gifts and character would make any but the most brash and race-conscious white man feel humble. Hertslet addressed him as Imbongi.

He came to the house that day because Hertslet had asked him to meet me. He wore European clothes as unwillingly as his nephew and as inappropriately, dressed as he was in a pair of trousers so much too large that they had to be hitched up almost to his armpits, a dark jacket and a woollen scarf—all this put on out of respect for the Doctor and his guest. He carried in one hand a ledger full of his industrious handwriting, and in the other his fortune-telling bag, every item of which and its significance he revealed to me later. It would have been worth while learning the Zulu language, I remember thinking, simply to hear him talk in his gentle yet confident voice. As it was I could only learn from him through the interpreting of his nephew.

He was not a tall man and was rather slightly built. He was perhaps forty years old and his hair, though thick, was receding from the temples. He wore a beard. But it was the eyes which would have made one notice him anywhere, large deep-set eyes under a high brow, eyes which gave him an expression of love and humour towards mankind; not satirical humour but kindly and full of understanding.

In his story was all the stoicism of the Zulu race and all its humiliations. In his attitude to white people, some of whom he had served, there was no suggestion of either bitterness or defiance. He treated me and Hertslet with candour and some affection; he would have treated an officious policeman with perhaps a touch of irony but without indignation.

He told me his story in which were alternations of humble employments and high Zulu office, not at all extraordinary while all his people are lumped together without distinction in white consideration as 'natives'. He was the son of Meseni, one of the leaders in the Zulu rising of 1906, and was born in the Chief's kraal at Emthandeni. He was taught—but not English, apparently—by Norwegian Lutherans and returned to Emthandeni to work as a wood-carver, being later employed in this capacity by a Durban furniture shop. He wrote Shembe hymns but was called by his brother Chief Mavutwa to act as treasurer and adviser at Emthandeni where he remained four years. He became a clerk in the Chief Native Commissioner's office in

Pietermaritzburg and was sent from there to settle difficulties in his tribe. He married Elizabeth Mfeka and enjoys a certain fame as a maker of Zulu poems.

He began to repeat his poem *The Tugela River* and there and then by the side of an earth track, which the three of us were following, I sat down and wrote a paraphrase of it from his nephew's translation.

A wonderful noise is made by the water under your banks
A rumbling noise, like thunder,
For you speak of conquest.
Consumer of all things
Drawing into yourself as you flow twisting and turning
The little streams from the mountains.
They come as if singing praises
As if you gave them organs of speech.

You drink and spit out again
The snake of countless heads,
Drawn into the sea and thrown out from you.

You are a snake covered by ripples from the swimming of
    sharks
With fangs like those of the red plant *lethangazan.*
Full of everlasting hatred
You cause the hatred in people
Because you saw and were made angry
By the Iziqoza army.

As we sleep you still sing the praises of victory
While the small streams flow into you,
Singing praises for your victory
In swallowing up the enemy army
Singing with wonderful repetition.

You made peace by throwing yourself
Between Mpande and Dingaan
During their marches in Zululand.
You separated the children of Mpande
You carried away Muyaze on your back
So that Cetywayo came and was crowned.
Snake lying coiled

Ready to strike at enemies
You rise in the hills like a spring
And draw in all people.

You flow swiftly with outspread wings
Seizing men and their weapons
Drawing them downwards
Never to rise again,
You echo the mourning of women with low voices
Like a tributary heard from a man's kraal on a hillside.

You are like an ox grazing on kikuyu grass
Which is poisonous to cattle and horses.

You are a path with no way over it.
You can only be crossed by a boat
From Chobeni, with smoke coming out of it
Crossing the bar on your shoulders.

Uncle and nephew were both moved by the recitation of this poem and sat for a long time while the nephew discussed the words of my paraphrase, trying to relate them exactly to his uncle's words.

But later when we had been given drinking water by a woman whose kraal was near our footpath we paused again, listening to a small Zulu goatherd playing a monotonous tune on a flute which he had carved for himself from a single white hollow stick, and Caleb diffidently approached his uncle Amos on the subject of his fortune-teller's bag. The older man agreed to tell my fortune, which he did by shaking the bag and after an incantation throwing out a number of objects and 'reading' them. The result was not impressive for I had known English gypsies who told much the same story after an examination of my palm. The preoccupations of more or less primitive people, when interpreted, are naive and irrelevant to us who demand something more sophisticated from our soothsayers than the prediction that someone beloved, now ill, will recover and that someone across the sea (in a place unimaginable by them) will be married before the new moon.

It was the objects themselves which interested me and after a moment's indecision Amos proceeded to state what these were and the precise significance for him of each of them. I list them in an Appendix and believe that as an example of Zulu magic practices the list is unique.

I wrote the list of objects on a writing-pad of lined paper which I had brought with me for this or a similar purpose. The paper has dried and yellowed and become dog-eared, for I carried it in a kitbag for several months and it has remained with me among old notes about Africa and some photographs, through all the vicissitudes and changes in my life. It has spent long periods in warehouses, has travelled to a good many countries until I have been able to dig it out from the past, here in Tunis where its details seem oddly at home.

When I had finished writing, we started to walk back to Mapamulo. I remember that as I walked between the two men I had a sense of wonder, not at what I had heard, or at the bare beautiful landscape, but that I should be here at all, free to move about and make notes concerning these strange people, free and enormously happy in the middle of a war, one campaign finished and another (as I thought) to come, free on a lonely African hillside, without the smallest semblance of care or responsibility. Next year I should be forty years old, I thought, and wondered if ever the shadows would gather or a time for reckoning close round me.

"Had a good day?" said Lewis Hertslet as we sat down to a satisfying meal with luscious fruit to end it.

Yes. I had had a good day.

CHAPTER ELEVEN
Mapamulo

[1]

I DO not know who first told me about John Dunn, an Englishman who lived among the Zulus through most of the last century, was decorated by Queen Victoria for his part in the Zulu War, and at the time of his death had forty-two wives and ninety-six children. The story fascinated me as I have always been fascinated by those exotic men and women who, coming from Victorian or pre-Victorian England, succeeded in creating for themselves a way of life of their own which only to their compatriots seemed eccentric, those travellers to the wilder shores of love and who were oblivious of conventions and fearless in the face of danger or derision, like Richard Burton, Roger Casement, Rajah Brooke or of an earlier age, Hester Stanhope.

I knew that John Dunn had been brought up in the English countryside and become a trapper in Natal. Moreover that he had as memorial an area of the country chiefly inhabited by the descendants and called Dunn's Reserve to this day. A subject for a book, I thought, which would absorb all my new-found interest in Zululand and the Zulus and have for its central subject a man worth writing about. I thought so for many years and although by now the book must have been written (though how adequately I do not know), I have sometimes had dreams of returning to the country and finding out the truth.

When I returned from Mapamulo to Durban I was full of it and enquired whether there was anyone living who had known John Dunn. Although I still went out to draw my pay from Clarewood Camp I had rented a garconnière in the town, a one-room apartment overlooking the sea which belonged to a schoolmistress now on holiday in Cape Town. I asked all my growing acquaintance about John Dunn and found them in no way surprised that I, who might get orders to embark for India at any moment, contemplated writing a book. Through one of them I met a senior policeman who in turn introduced me to Colonel Henry Sparks, now in his nineties, who had known John Dunn as intimately as anyone. It was kindness on the part of Sparks to let me ask him questions—he was at that time in a wheelchair and although his memory had not altogether failed, it was often slow to connect. He had served in the Natal Mounted Rifles in both the Zulu War and the Boer War and recalled both, but he had never been asked about his acquaintance with John Dunn and although at first he spoke feebly and indifferently, his memory quickened as he talked.

He spoke chiefly of Dunn's markmanship which was phenomenal, and there were the usual stories of improbable *safari* feats including one, which Sparks maintained vehemently, that Dunn had shot a crocodile forty-two feet long.* Dunn owed his friendship with Cetewayo to his feat in shooting five lions.

I had to glean what facts I could from the old Colonel, just as he remembered things. To ask questions was to put him off.

Dunn first married a half-caste, he said, Catherine Pierce, the mother of Mary Rose and Jane Sunny Dunn, but for years he was one of only a handful of settlers and hunters in the whole country (after Dingaan had massacred the Dutch settlers) and took to polygamy as a matter of course.

He had fine spans of oxen, fourteen to eighteen in a span, always matching, dun-coloured being his favourite. He would come down by waggon every year to Durban and purchase a gift for each of his children and grandchildren.

---

*Encyclopaedia Britannica says that it is difficult to know the maximum length of crocodiles owing to the number of exaggerated stories with wide currency. 'The largest species is the salt-water or estuarine crocodile which reaches a length of more than 20 ft.'

He was, said Sparks, a quiet, dignified, reserved man who never discussed his patriarchal family life. He was popular and respected by the Europeans whom he would invite to visit him up country. He kept a guest-house prepared in each of his kraals and lived in considerable state with a good table and fine wines.

Sparks remembered only two remarks of Dunn's. One was made to some settlers or missionaries who had dared touch on the size of his family. "I have forty wives," he said, "and can trust them all. You have one apiece and daren't let them out of your sight." The other remark was a more serious one, for when speaking of an ultimatum he said—"It was never given. It would have cost a man's life."

This outsize figure appears in history when during the Zulu War of 1879 with the tragedy of Rorkesdrift, and Lord Chelmsford's victory at Ulundi, Sir Garnet Wolseley allowed the country to drift into civil war between the followers of Cetewayo and those of Zibebu. Wolseley assigned the land between the Tugela and the Umlatusi rivers to John Dunn, to keep as a reserve, a haven and a buffer. Later Dunn supported Zibebu, whom Sparks described as a fine man and a soldier, against Cetewayo's son Dinizulu, who attacked and routed him with a group of Boers from the Transvaal.

What the ancient Colonel told me increased my appetite for information and it was reported to Killie Campbell, the owner of the finest (bar the Oppenheimers') collection of Africana which then existed. She gave me the freedom of her library and I spent several days there before Christmas, but realized the hopelessness of trying to complete a biography with so much historical detail in it, during a month or two of freedom, itself a lucky chance, in wartime.

[2]

As Christmas approached I learned from one of the Gunner

officers who had been with us in Madagascar of his dilemma over Eddy Pierce, a half-negro Londoner in their battery. After a disturbing experience in a pub on our first night in Durban, Eddy had kept to himself. Every other man in the Madagascar Force had gone on leave, invited by hospitable Europeans, but there had been no leave for Eddy whose colour precluded him from white houses and whose British birth and upbringing gave him no point of conflict with Black Africa. I at once thought of Father L'Hôte in the Mapamulo Mission and wrote to him to explain the problem. That dear old saintly man wrote back and said that of course Eddy would be welcome at the Mission and that he hoped we would both spend Christmas there. So we went up from Stanger by the same rattling bus and were met at Mapamulo by two young Zulus of Father L'Hôte's congregation who had brought horses for us. We mounted these, sturdy ponies who were accustomed to the journey, and set out through the dusk, the young men trotting behind us. It was not a great distance, three or four miles as I remember it, but we had to ford a river which was running quite high and it all seemed very adventurous.

The Mission came in sight high on a hill. The horses cantered towards it and the two Zulus, having brought us safely to our goal, fell behind. Father L'Hôte, the great white beard which covered his chest visible from a long way off, welcomed us and took us in to dinner at once. The table like all the furniture had been made at the Mission itself from local wood. It was rough but laid with French neatness and propriety. And though the meal was simple, it too was in some indefinable way French, from its bounteous plate of soup to its well-arranged fruit.

One of the boys who had brought the horses was named Philip Kumalo and hoped to be a priest. He spoke good mission-school English and on Christmas Eve volunteered to take us in the afternoon to visit some of the kraals in the neighbourhood. He wore European clothes, for Father L'Hôte had taught him that it was 'wrong to expose the body', a piece of doctrine not easy to put over among the Zulus, I should have thought. Philip viewed my interest in his people and their homes and customs with cynicism, though he was always amiable and obliging. *He* had grown out of all that barbarism, he seemed to say, and thought my collection of beadwork ornaments childish and my taste for Zulu beer and dances retrograde and unspiritual.

But he led us over the hills as Caleb Gumede had done a month or two earlier, and perhaps because people in the Mission area lived more remotely, they seemed to have lost less to civilization. We went to the kraal of an old wood-carver who was smoking powdered hemp on charcoal from a primitive hubble-bubble made from a cow's horn, inhaling it with open mouth over the wide end of the horn which had a bowl inserted by a trumpet mouthpiece. He had five noisy wives and a wound in his leg from fighting in Bambata's Rebellion in 1907 which, he insisted, was before I was born. He had cow-hide mats set for us to sit on and gave us some particularly good Zulu beer, but the inside of his hut was crawling with insects and hung with smoke-blackened corn-cobs and berries. He accepted some sweets, 'for the children' he said, though there was no sign of any, and with great joy, a box of matches.

Another kraal was that of Mkewu, the acting chief. He saw us from a hilltop and hurried down to greet us, a handsome old man of keen intelligence who gave us a choice of seats, chairs or mats and seemed delighted when we chose mats. We walked home briskly through mealy patches by footpaths from kraal to kraal and came on a crowd of little boys roasting meat. At the sight of us they ran to cover but returned for a gift of sweets. A crowd of women coming from the store were scarcely less shy, covering their faces as they passed.

We returned long before midnight, when Father L'Hôte was to say Mass. I have heard Midnight Mass on Christmas Eve in some pretty strange places and among people not otherwise noted for their piety, but this was the most bizarre occasion of all. The church itself had been built by the hands which were now holding the chalice, and the altar-cloth and vestments had been worked by the women in the aisles. Every cement block had been carried on the heads of Zulus from five miles away when Father L'Hôte had been a young man. The congregation of today numbered two hundred or more, the women dressed in store-house finery, the men in trousers and shirts. Many of the families had walked ten miles or more and would stay at the Mission for Mass next morning, but these were not as many in numbers as the large crowd outside the church who wore no store clothes, or indeed anything beyond a loin-cloth, who had never been taught Christian doctrines, who came not to hear Mass but to be near the scene of this marvellous occasion, the fame of which had reached them in distant kraals. They did not try to enter, they did not understand the strange singing that came from within, but they believed, or so Philip Kumalo told me with disgust, that some good would come to them as a result of their attendance here, that some magic was generated from the white-haired priest's incantations. The singing was powerful from both men and women and we approached the Crib with carols sung with Zulu words, *Silent Night* and *Adeste Fideles*.

Bizarre? Yes, but moving, too. The light of lanterns outside the church fell on the black eyes and half-naked figures of those who could not enter but crowded round the doors waiting for some mysterious benediction which they did not understand. The music from the choir was not the music, familiar and some-times monotonous, which they knew, but alien and disquieting to them. They waited through the Mass; when we went to bed they remained huddled under the trees and when we woke in the morning sunlight they were there still.

But for Eddy and me, who were after all soldiers accustomed to scrounging for whatever good things might come our way, the dinner which was provided that Christmas Day had its importance, too. Roast goose, wine and sweet things in great variety the old priest offered us with the naive pride of one who wanted to give pleasures in which he could not share.

[3]

I never grew tired of visiting the kraals in each of which there was something different to see, or observing the dignity and warmth with which they welcomed me after they had been told that I was not a policeman or any kind of official, but an English soldier from overseas who asked for nothing but their friendship. Of those days at Mapamulo and in the country round I have too many small memories to chronicle but they seem precious to me now that I have come so far in time and distance.

I remember that on the afternoon of Christmas Day I went with Eddy and Philip Kumalo to what can only be described as a party of younger people and there was dancing inside a hut and I could watch from close the astonishing movements, the flash of leg in that terrific downward kick that resounded with a smack of the naked foot, the swagger, the twist, the almost maniacal violence of the dance.

I remember too one of those interminable treks across country with Caleb Gumede, who was untirable, to the kraal described as the royal kraal of his tribe, the Qwabe or Gumede, at Emthandeni, in which Amos Gumede had been born, the son of the Chief Masena who had been exiled to St Helena. Masena had five sons, the father and four uncles of Caleb Gumede. The nominal Chief was one of these, Mtshingwa, but was mildly insane. Although the revenues were paid to him his brother Pumezinhleni Kameseni Gumede was the administrative head of the tribe since another brother, Mavutwa, had left the kraal to become a prison warder in government service. Yet another brother was Pumekufeni, and the fifth was Amos Hlalehlathani Kumede, the *imbongi* met at Mapamulo who had revealed the secrets of his fortune-telling bag.

Lemon trees had been planted near the kraal, 'so that we can give our friends a drink', and a drink of sweet refreshing lemonade was produced. Pumezinhleni told me that his father Maseni, a leader in the Zulu Rebellion of 1906, had told him on his

death-bed always to respect the English. This had surprised his
son who knew of his father's imprisonment and exile. "Why?"
he asked. "Because the people of any other race would have
executed me."

Philip Kumalo asked us to *his* kraal, that of the Induna
Magemegeme Ngcobo, of the Amaqadi tribe. (How carefully I
noted the names and titles of them all, whom I have never seen
or heard of since that Christmas week.) The older men here
talked of the past and because I was an Englishman told me of
the British officers who had fought them in the Zulu Rising of
1906. Perhaps none of them had followed young Philip to
Christianity and education (almost synonymous in Zululand),
and he was proud of his own hut with its books and framed
photographs of Mission groups, and a German beer-mug
musical-box which played two tunes, while seeming perfectly
at home among his untutored elders.

[4]

That was all I saw of Zululand and within a week of returning to Durban I was ordered to go on board a troopship
bound for India. There remains a collection of bead ornaments
in brilliant colours, seeming as I write like exhibits in a junk
shop, though they were collected with immense satisfaction
during those weeks in Zululand, and I learned the import of
their designs, for each square of beads with its geometrical
pattern conveyed a message from the girl who worked it to the
man to whom it was given. The early traders brought beads to
tempt the Africans with their bright colours, and from them
they have created a little art in its own right. Beads, a few
photographs, odds and ends of knowledge and some vivid
memories, but I would have been poorer without them and
shall perhaps be poorer now because I shall lose possession of
them by writing them away here.

[5]

The journey from Durban to Bombay was the last I should make with the RSFs, for when I arrived in India I should go from the public bar of the Army to the saloon by obtaining a commission and becoming a Field Security Officer, that anomalous rank with its extraordinary freedoms and its illusions at least of being useful. I have written of that in *The Gorgeous East,* which chronologically follows this book though it was written before it. I enjoyed it, of course; I enjoy everything; but it had not those alliterative qualities, variety, vitality, virility (verve too, if you like), of my years among the licentious soldiery. It even made me conscientious, at times, a sorry state for a soldier, and almost succeeded in giving me a sense of responsibility. But I never again played 'Ha'penny Brag' or drank my tot at noon, or swore like a trooper, or vowed eternal friendships which would last at least a month till an order came to move, or felt myself as bad as the next man and gloried in it.

Appendix

The bones of a sheep with a string of white beads round it:
  this signifies the person whose fortune is being told.
The same with green beads: his or her brother.
3 bones of a ram: brother-in-law.
3 bones of a young nanny-goat: unmarried girls.
1 bone of an old nanny-goat: a married woman.
1 bone of a black ram: the prevention of evil spirits.
1 bone of an old nanny-goat: the work of other Diviners.
2 bones of a young ram which have been given to a diviner:
  signifies the person of another diviner.
1 bone of a young nanny-goat which had died of disease:
  signifies disease.
3 bones of a young billy-goat: boys.
1 bone of a goat which had been killed for feast of ancestors:
  ancestors.
1 bone of a spring-bok: a cruel person.
1 bone of a buck: bad luck.
1 bone of a very old billy-goat: an old man.
1 bone of a very old nanny-goat: an old woman.
1 bone of a very old bull: an ox to be slaughtered.
1 bone of a baboon: a diviner who is remaining hidden but
  working against you.
1 bone of a young calf which has died a natural death: family
  dying.
1 bone of a donkey: disease called *ufufunyana*.
1 bone of a rabbit: person who runs away.
1 bone of a mamba: stomach disease.

1 bone of a calf before its time: woman in child-birth.

1 bone of a cobra: the dead.

1 bone of a sea fish: disease in ribs.

2 flat stones: stomach disease.

1 round stone: the way you are going.

1 round stone: the heart.

1 round stone: impure blood.

1 flat stone: bad blood.

2 round stones: good medicine recently used.

1 stone from the bed of a big river: a person who is behaving badly.

1 head of a glass dog, piece broken from a small ornament: means nightmare.

1 electric light-bulb: evil spirits which show a light—lucifer, I suppose, or will o' the wisps.

1 big ring, though any ring will serve: the bladder.

1 string of white beads: love.

1 small string of white beads: good luck.

1 string of white and black beads: good and evil thoughts.

1 string of grey beads: antiquity.

1 string of red beads: the human heart.

1 string of yellow beads: a strong body.

1 piece of brass: the human head.

1 piece of a pen: writing.

1 religious medal: a judge.

1 piece of glass: fear.

1 wheel of a watch, though any wheel will do: palpitations.

1 draught: disease of hernia.

1 2s. piece: a large inheritance.

1 6d. piece: a small inheritance.

1 piece of a tortoise-shell: disease in the head.

1 human tooth: tooth-ache.

1 piece of wood: luck.

3 pieces of soft wood: diseases said to be caused by other sorcerers.

4 pieces of wood which mean severally: 1 disease sent by evil

spirits. 2 poison being administered by women. 3 danger approaching. 4 disease.

2 pieces of pottery: unexpected happenings.

Besides all these there were altogether 24 sea shells, each distinguishable, and each with a different significance. Their meanings were as follows: the human hand, the kraal, disease of the lungs, a Diviner, disease, fear, a rash spreading over the body, disease among women, an event in the night, the truth, the moon or one month, the disease of Bilharzia (bellhousia), a female child, a small baby, a girl recently in love, a girl engaged to be married, an unmarried mother, women of the kraal, dreams, a child's foot, an old person's foot, an assegai, a town.

There were two shells whose significance depended on which side was upwards when they fell. One meant good luck one side up, bad luck the reverse. The other shell signified gossip if it fell one way. If it fell the other, the grave.

Finally there was the bone of a bird whose flight is supposed to cause thunderstorms, the *inyoniyezulu* bird: bewitched, or struck by lightning.

The method of using the bag varies with each diviner. Amos Gumede shakes it several times and invokes it to speak the truth and reveal what he wants to know. He then throws out the contents and proceeds to read the future from the way in which the various articles have fallen.

B